A DREAM TOO WILD

*Emerson Meditations
for Every Day of the Year*

Edited by
Barry M. Andrews

SKINNER HOUSE BOOKS
BOSTON

Printed in Canada

Cover design by Kimberly Glyder
Text design by Sandra Rigney

ISBN 1-55896-452-5

Library of Congress Cataloging-in-Publication Data

Emerson, Ralph Waldo, 1803–1882.
    A dream too wild : a book of meditations from the writ-
ings of Ralph Waldo Emerson for every day of the year /
[edited by] Barry M. Andrews.
        p. cm.
    Includes bibliographical references.
    ISBN 1-55896-452-5 (alk. paper)
    1. Devotional calendars. I. Andrews, Barry Maxwell. II.
Title

BV4811.E48 2003
814'.3—dc21   2003042723

10 9 8 7 6 5 4 3 2 1
06 05 04 03

Please see the last page for acknowledgment of copyrighted
material.

To my mother, Judith,
who first taught me self-reliance.

INTRODUCTION

Emerson is the most quoted of American writers. He was a master of the aphorism. Familiar passages fill eight pages of my copy of *Bartlett's Quotations*. Yet, curiously, there have been few anthologies of his sayings and, to my knowledge, none quite like this one. Those that have been published are typically brief quotes on a variety of topics. The problem with these is that the sentences quoted are not sufficient to convey the texture and nuance of the thought process that occasioned them in the first place.

Moreover, in spite of the fact that Emerson wrote and lectured on many subjects, he was essentially a spiritual writer. In his journal he insisted that he had taught but one doctrine, namely, the infinitude of the individual person. His audiences accepted the doctrine readily enough when it was expressed in terms of art or politics or literature, but were shocked the moment he called it religion, though that is in fact what it was. One cannot read any of his essays without failing to notice the essentially spiritual message that lies at the heart of his philosophy.

It is Emerson's spiritual vision that is reflected in the selections chosen for this book of meditations, one for every day of the year. These represent the full range of his thought on spiritual maters, including his ideas on nature, self-reliance, the over-soul, compensation, the moral sentiment, solitude, "plain living and high thinking," ecstasy, polarity or undulation, and the nature and means of self-culture. Moreover, they are drawn from every period of his life, from his youthful idealism to the wisdom of experience in later life.

This book of meditations is also unique in that, with the exception of his correspondence, it draws from his entire published writings—his early sermons and lectures, his journals, his many volumes of books and essays, his poetry and, with their publication only last year, his later lectures as well.

Emerson was a prolific writer, but by his own admission, he was not a systematic thinker. To be sure, there is a theme or argument to each of his essays and lectures, and they are best read entire. However, as his readers and auditors well knew, it was Emerson's practice to string his thoughts together like beads on a necklace. The passages included here represent the beads of Emerson's thoughts on spiritual issues. Each one, long or short, contains a "lustre," as he called it, a thought to ponder, a brief meditation to contemplate.

He intended to be provocative and made it clear that he spoke only for himself. But he also believed that genius or inspiration was everywhere the same and that what was true for us in our heart of hearts was likely to be true for others as well. If he was provocative, it was with the intention of waking people up. More than anything else he sought to excite the soul.

Emerson was very much a person of his era, but his thought is timeless because it partakes of the perennial wisdom that has permeated philosophy and religion in every age and culture. Emerson continues to be relevant because, as he said of himself, "I am an endless seeker with no past at my back." Spiritual seekers of this and coming ages will continue to find in Emerson a kindred soul.

JANUARY

Meditations

JANUARY 1

We are always getting ready to live, but never living. We have many years of technical education; then, many years of earning a livelihood, and we get sick, and take journeys for our health, and compass land and sea for improvement by traveling, but the work of self-improvement—always under the nose,—nearer than the nearest, is seldom...engaged in. A few, few hours in the longest life. Set out to study a particular truth. Read upon it. Walk to think upon it. Talk of it. Write about it. The thing itself will not much manifest itself, at least not much in accommodation to your studying arrangements. The gleams you do get, out they will flash, as likely at dinner, or in the roar of Faneuil Hall, as in your painfullest abstraction. Very little life in a lifetime.

—JOURNAL, 1834

How many hours do you suppose you have lived? Can you think of a time when you pondered a question the answer to which came at an unlikely time or place?

JANUARY 2

We are like children who repeat by rote the sentences of grandames and tutors, and, as they grow older, of the men of talents and character they chance to see,—painfully recollecting the exact words they spoke; afterwards, when they come into the point of view which those had who uttered these sayings, they understand them, and are willing to let the words go; for, at any time, they can use words as good when occasion comes. If we live truly, we shall see truly. It is as easy for the strong man to be strong, as it is for the weak to be weak. When we have new perception, we shall gladly disburden the memory of its hoarded treasures as old rubbish. When a man lives with God, his voice shall be as sweet as the murmur of the brook and the rustle of the corn.

—Self-Reliance

As you grow older, do you have less need to rely on the thinking of others? What does it mean to "live truly"?

JANUARY 3

Will you offer empires to such as cannot set a house or private affairs in order? Here are people who cannot dispose of a day; an hour hangs heavy on their hands; and will you offer them rolling ages without end? But this is the way we rise. Within every man's thought is a higher thought,—within the character he exhibits today, a higher character. The youth puts off the illusions of the child, the man puts off the ignorance and tumultuous passions of youth; proceeding thence puts off the egotism of manhood, and becomes at last a public and universal soul. He is rising to greater heights, but also rising to realities; the outer regions and circumstances dying out, he entering deeper into God, God into him, until the last garment of egotism falls, and he is with God,—shares the will and the immensity of the First Cause.

—IMMORTALITY

Can you dispose of a day? Do you think you are rising to greater heights in regard to your spiritual life?

JANUARY 4

One would think from the talk of men, that riches and poverty were a great matter; and our civilization mainly respects it. But the Indians say, that they do not think the white man with his brow of care, always toiling, afraid of heat and cold, and keeping within doors, has any advantage of them. The permanent interest of every man is, never to be in a false position, but to have the weight of Nature to back him in all that he does. Riches and poverty are a thick or thin costume; and our life— the life of all of us—identical. For we transcend the circumstance continually, and taste the real quality of existence; as in our employments, which only differ in the manipulations, but express the same laws; or in our thoughts, which wear no silks, and taste no ice-creams. We see God face to face every hour, and know the savor of Nature.

—Illusions

What would it take to have "the weight of Nature" behind you? What is "the real quality of existence"? Have you experienced it?

JANUARY 5

Man is a stream whose source is hidden. Our being is descending into us from we know not whence. The most exact calculator has no prescience that somewhat incalculable may not balk the very next moment. I am constrained every moment to acknowledge a higher origin for events than the will I call mine. As with events, so is it with thoughts. When I watch that flowing river, which, out of regions I see not, pours for a season its streams into me, I see that I am a pensioner; not a cause, but a surprised spectator of this ethereal water; that I desire and look up, and put myself in the attitude of reception, but from some alien energy the visions come.

—THE OVER-SOUL

Do you acknowledge "a higher origin for events" than your own will? Do you set aside time to put yourself "in the attitude of reception"?

JANUARY 6

I can very confidently announce one or another law, which throws itself into relief and form, but I am too young yet by some ages to compile a code. I gossip for my hour concerning the eternal politics. I have seen many fair pictures not in vain. A wonderful time I have lived in. I am not the novice I was fourteen, nor yet seven years ago. Let who will ask, where is the fruit? I find a private fruit sufficient. This is a fruit,—that I should not ask for a rash effect from meditations, counsels, and the hiving of truths. I should feel it pitiful to demand a result on this town and country, an overt effect on the instant month and year. The effect is deep and secular as the cause. It works on periods in which mortal lifetime is lost. All I know is reception; I am and I have: but I do not get, and when I have fancied I had gotten anything, I found I did not. I worship with wonder the great Fortune.

—Experience

What are some of the fruits of your spiritual quest? How would you characterize your own journey?

JANUARY 7

That which befits us, embosomed in beauty and wonder as we are, is cheerfulness and courage, and the endeavor to realize our aspirations. The life of man is the true romance, which, when it is valiantly conducted, will yield the imagination a higher joy than any fiction. All around us, what powers are wrapped up under the coarse mattings of custom, and all wonder prevented. It is so wonderful to our neurologists that a man can see without his eyes, that it does not occur to them, that it is just as wonderful, that he should see with them; and that is ever the difference between the wise and the unwise: the latter wonders at what is unusual, the wise man wonders at the usual. Shall not the heart which has received so much, trust the Power by which it lives? May it not quit other leadings, and listen to the Soul that has guided it so gently, and taught it so much, secure that the future will be worthy of the past?

—New England Reformers

What are some of the "mattings of custom" that keep you from seeing the beauty and wonder of life? Do you find wonder in the ordinary?

JANUARY 8

The peculiarity of divine souls is shown by Parmenides, to consist in their being younger, and at the same time older both than themselves, and other things. Every man has had one or two moments of extraordinary experience, has met his soul, has thought of something which he never afterwards forgot and which revised all his speech and moulded all his forms of thought. A perfect resignation was with every want and every loss. None was so ardent in loving and admiring Genius. He could feel its influence on each hour of his life. He knows he does not exist so largely as these benefactors, but his own few prized thoughts were never sacrileged by soliciting for them the sympathy of crowds. Besides, it is the purpose of the great ordainer, whom he adores, who could endow him as highly as those he admires, were it best.

—Essential Principles of Religion

Have you had "one or two moments of extraordinary experience"? How did they change your life?

JANUARY 9

Yes, we have a pretty artillery of tools now in our social arrangements: we ride four times as fast as our fathers did; travel, grind, weave, forge, plant, till and excavate better. We have new shoes, gloves, glasses and gimlets; we have the calculus; we have the newspaper, which does its best to make every square acre of land and sea give an account of itself at your breakfast table; we have money, and paper money; we have language,—the finest tool of all, and nearest to the mind. Much will have more. Man flatters himself that his command over Nature must increase. Things begin to obey him.... Tantalus, who in old times was seen vainly trying to quench his thirst with a flowing stream which ebbed whenever he approached it, has been seen again lately. He is in Paris, in New York, in Boston. He is now in great spirits; thinks he shall reach it yet; thinks he shall bottle the wave. It is however getting a little doubtful.... No matter how many centuries of culture have preceded, the new man always finds himself standing on the brink of chaos, always in crisis.

—WORKS AND DAYS

Today our "pretty artillery of tools" includes cell phones and the Internet. Has the situation Emerson describes changed much since his time? Are you able to moderate your own desires?

JANUARY 10

Let Christianity speak ever for the poor and the low. Though the voice of society should demand a defense of slavery from all its organs that service can never be expected from me. My opinion is of no worth, but I have not a syllable of all the language I have learned, to utter for the planter. If by opposing slavery I go to undermine institutions I confess I do not wish to live in a nation where slavery exists. The life of this world has but a limited worth in my eyes and really is not worth such a price as the toleration of slavery. Therefore though I may be so far restrained by unwillingness to cut the planter's throat as that I should refrain from denouncing him, yet I pray God that not even in my dream or in madness may I ever incur the disgrace of articulating one word of apology for the slave-trader or slave-holder.

—JOURNAL, 1835

Have you ever opposed society and its institutions on the basis of conscience? What issues engage your conscience today? What have you done about them?

JANUARY 11

Do not trifle with your perceptions, or hold them cheap. They are your door to the seven heavens, and if you pass it by you will miss your way. Say what impresses me ought to impress me. I am bewildered by the immense variety of attractions and cannot take a step; but this one thread, fine as gossamer, is yet real; and I hear a whisper, which I dare trust, that it is the thread on which the earth and the heaven of heavens are strung. The universe is traversed by paths or bridges or stepping-stones across the gulfs of space in every direction. To every soul that is created is its path, invisible to all but itself. Each soul, therefore, walking in its own path walks firmly; and to the astonishment of all other souls, who see not its path, it goes as softly and playfully on its way as if, instead of being a line, narrow as the edge of a sword, over terrific pits right and left, it were a wide prairie.

—NATURAL HISTORY OF INTELLECT

What are the stepping-stones that mark your spiritual path? How would you describe the thread of your life on which earth and heaven are strung?

JANUARY 12

But the final value of action, like that of books, and better than books, is, that it is a resource. That great principle of Undulation in nature, that shows itself in the inspiring and expiring of the breath; in desire and satiety; in the ebb and flow of the sea; in day and night; in heat and cold; and as yet more deeply ingrained in every atom and every fluid, is known to us under the name of Polarity,—these "fits of easy transmission and reflection," as Newton called them, are the law of nature because they are the law of spirit. The mind now thinks; now acts; and each fit reproduces the other. When the artist has exhausted his materials, when the fancy no longer paints, when thoughts are no longer apprehended, and books are a weariness,—he has always the resource to live. Character is higher than intellect. Thinking is the function. Living is the functionary. The stream retreats to its source. A great soul will be strong to live, as well as strong to think. Does he lack organ or medium to impart his truths? He can still fall back on this elemental force of living them. This is a total act. Thinking is a partial act.

—THE AMERICAN SCHOLAR

Have you ever exhausted your "materials"? What did you do about it? Do you think character is higher than intellect?

JANUARY 13

Let us draw a lesson from nature, which always works by short ways. When the fruit is ripe, it falls. When the fruit is dispatched, the leaf falls. The circuit of the waters is mere falling. The walking of man and all animals is a falling forward. All our manual labor and works of strength, as prying, splitting, digging, rowing, and so forth, are done by dint of continual falling, and the globe, earth, moon, comet, sun, star, fall for ever and ever. The simplicity of the universe is very different from the simplicity of a machine. He who sees moral nature out and out, and thoroughly knows how knowledge is acquired and character formed, is a pedant. The simplicity of nature is not that which may easily be read, but is inexhaustible. The last analysis can no wise be made.

—Spiritual Laws

Do you find wisdom for your own spiritual life in the lesson Emerson draws from nature? Do you find most moralists to be pedants?

JANUARY 14

Of course, it needs the whole society, to give the symmetry we seek. The parti-colored wheel must revolve very fast to appear white. Something is learned too by conversing with so much folly and defect. In fine, whoever loses, we are always of the gaining party. Divinity is behind our failures and follies also. The plays of children are nonsense, but very educative nonsense. So it is with the largest and solemnest things, with commerce, government, church, marriage, and so with the history of every man's bread, and the ways by which he is to come by it. Like a bird which alights nowhere, but hops perpetually from bough to bough, is the Power which abides in no man and in no woman, but for a moment speaks from this one, and for another moment from that one.

— EXPERIENCE

What have you learned from your failures? How do your successes and failures contribute to the whole of society?

JANUARY 15

We are born believing. A man bears beliefs, as a tree bears apples....I and my neighbors have been bred in the notion, that, unless we came soon to some good church,—Calvinism, or Behmenism, or Romanism, or Mormanism,—there would be a universal thaw and dissolution....The stern old faiths have all pulverized. 'Tis a whole population of gentlemen and ladies out in search of religions. 'Tis as flat anarchy in our ecclesiastic realms, as that which existed in Massachusetts, in the Revolution, or which prevails now on the slope of the Rocky Mountains or Pike's Peak. Yet we make shift to live. Men are loyal. Nature has self-poise in all her works; certain proportions in which oxygen and azote combine, and, not less a harmony in faculties, a fitness in the spring and regulator. The decline of the influence of Calvin, or Fenelon, or Wesley, or Channing, need give us no uneasiness. The builder of heaven has not so ill constructed his creature as that the religion, that is, the public nature, should fall out: the public and the private element, like north and south, like inside and outside, like centrifugal and centripetal, adhere to every soul, and cannot be subdued, except the soul is dissipated. God builds his temple in the heart on the ruins of churches and religions.

— WORSHIP

Were you "born believing"? If so, is your religion an adequate representation of the faith you were born with?

JANUARY 16

There is a certain Beatitude,—I can call it nothing less,—to which all men are entitled, tasted by them in different degrees, which is a perfection of their nature, and to which their entrance must be in every way forwarded. Practical men, though they could lift the globe, cannot arrive at this. Something very different from their feats has to be done, the availing ourselves of every impulse of genius,—an emanation of the heaven it tells of,—and the resisting this conspiracy of men and of material things against the salutary and legitimate inspirations of the intellectual nature: and, though to make an apology for the Intellect, may seem to be like drawing with chalk on white paper, I must risk the speaking of the excellency of that Element.

—THE POWERS AND LAWS OF THOUGHT

Have you tasted the beatitude Emerson describes in this passage? Do you trust your own intelligence?

JANUARY 17

As long as the soul seeks an external God, it can never have peace, it always must be uncertain what may be done and what may become of it. But when it sees the Great God far within its own nature, then it sees that always itself is a party to all that can be, that always it will be informed of that which will happen and therefore it is pervaded with a great peace. The individual is always dying. The Universal is life. As much truth and goodness enters into me, so much I live. As much error and sin, so much death is in me.

—JOURNAL, 1836

Where, if anywhere, do you see God? Do you find the universal coming to life in you?

JANUARY 18

The problem of restoring to the world original and eternal beauty, is solved by the redemption of the soul. The ruin or the blank, that we see when we look at nature, is in our own eye. The axis of vision is not coincident with the axis of things, and so they appear not transparent but opaque. The reason why the world lacks unity, and lies broken and in heaps, is because man is disunited with himself. He cannot be a naturalist, until he satisfies all the demands of the spirit.

—NATURE

Are we disunited with ourselves? Do our problems lie in our lack of perception?

Meantime, whilst the doors of the temple stand open, night and day, before every man, and the oracles of this truth cease never, it is guarded by one stern condition; this, namely; it is an intuition. It cannot be received at second hand. Truly speaking, it is not instruction, but provocation, that I can receive from another soul. What he announces, I must find true in me, or wholly reject; and on his word, or as his second, be he who he may, I can accept nothing. On the contrary, the absence of this primary faith is the presence of degradation. As is the flood so is the ebb. Let this faith depart, and the very words it spake, and the things it made, become false and hurtful. Then falls the church, the state, art, letters, life. The doctrine of the divine nature being forgotten, a sickness infects and dwarfs the constitution. Once man was all; now he is an appendage, a nuisance. And because the indwelling Supreme Spirit cannot wholly be got rid of, the doctrine of it suffers this perversion, that the divine nature is attributed to one or two persons, and denied to all the rest, and denied with fury. The doctrine of inspiration is lost; the base doctrine of the majority of voices, usurps the place of the doctrine of the soul. Miracles, prophecy, poetry; the ideal life, the holy life, exist as ancient history merely; they are not in the belief, nor in the aspiration of society; but, when suggested, seem ridiculous. Life is comic or pitiful, as soon as the high ends of being fade out of sight, and man becomes near-sighted, and can only attend to what addresses the senses.

— THE DIVINITY SCHOOL ADDRESS

What is the basis of religion for you? Intellect? The senses? Intuition?

JANUARY 20

Achilles is not quite invulnerable; the sacred waters did not wash the heel by which Thetis held him. Siegfried, in the Nibelungen, is not quite immortal, for a leaf fell on his back whilst he was bathing in the dragon's blood, and that spot which it covered is mortal. And so it must be. There is a crack in every thing God has made. It would seem, there is always this vindictive circumstance stealing in at unawares, even into the wild poesy in which the human fancy attempted to make bold holiday, and to shake itself free of the old laws,—this back-stroke, this kick of the gun, certifying that the law is fatal; that in nature nothing can be given, all things are sold.

—Compensation

Is there truth in the myths and legends of heroes with a vulnerable spot? Do you have an Achilles' heel? What does it mean that "in nature nothing can be given, all things are sold"?

JANUARY 21

Life is a series of surprises. We do not guess today the mood, the pleasure, the power of tomorrow, when we are building up our being.... The one thing which we seek with insatiable desire is to forget ourselves, to be surprised out of our propriety, to lose our sempiternal memory, and to do something without knowing how or why; in short, to draw a new circle. Nothing great was ever achieved without enthusiasm. The way of life is wonderful: it is by abandonment. The great moments of history are the facilities of performance through the strength of ideas, as the works of genius and religion.... Dreams and drunkenness, the use of opium and alcohol are the semblance and counterfeit of this oracular genius, and hence their dangerous attraction for men. For the like reason, they ask the aid of wild passions, as in gaming and war, to ape in some manner these flames and generosities of the heart.

—CIRCLES

What are you enthusiastic about? Do you agree with Emerson that the way of life is "by abandonment"?

The revelation of Thought takes man out of servitude into freedom. We rightly say of ourselves, we were born, and afterward we were born again, and many times. We have successive experiences so important, that the new forgets the old, and hence the mythology of the seven or the nine heavens. The day of days, the great day of the feast of life, is that in which the inward eye opens to the Unity in things, to the omnipresence of law;—sees that what is must be, and ought to be, or is the best. This beatitude dips from on high down on us, and we see. It is not in us so much as we are in it. If the air come to our lungs, we breathe and live; if not, we die. If the light come to our eyes, we see; else not. And if truth come to our mind, we suddenly expand to its dimensions, as if we grew to worlds. We are as lawgivers; we speak for Nature; we prophesy and divine.

—FATE

How many times have you been born? Have you experienced "the great day of the feast of life"?

All the senses minister to a mind which they do not know. The eye does not see it, the ear does not hear it, the nose does not smell it; the tongue does not taste it; nor the hand touch it; but the mind residing in the body, and giving it all its force, is a force hidden to everything below it. These senses that feed it know no more of it than the granite mountain or the heaving sea do. All things are full of Jove. You cannot exaggerate the powers of the mind. All that the world admires comes from within: in other words, our whole existence is subjective. What we are, that we see, love, hate. A man externalizes himself in his friends, in his enemies... in his aims, in his actions, in his fortunes, and in his religion. 'Tis the fullness of man that runs over into objects, and makes his bibles, and Shakespeares, and Homers so great. The joyful reader borrows of his own ideas to fill their faulty outline, and knows not that he borrows and gives.

—POWERS OF THE MIND

How do you affect your surroundings? Which do you trust more in your spiritual life, your senses or your intellect?

JANUARY 24

Is it not true that contemplation belongs to us and therefore outward worship *because* our reason is at discord with our understanding? And that whenever we live rightly thought will express itself in ordinary action so fully as to make a special action, that is, a religious form impertinent?...Is not the meeting-house dedicated because men are not? Is not the Church opened and filled on Sunday because the commandments are not kept by the worshippers on Monday? But when he who worships there, speaks the truth, follows the truth, is the truth's; when he awakes by actual communion to the faith that God is in him, will he need any temple, any prayer?...Now does this sound like high treason and go to lay flat all religion?...It threatens our forms but it does not touch injuriously Religion. Would there be danger if there were real religion? If the doctrine that God is in man were faithfully taught and received, if I lived to speak the truth and enact it, if I pursued every generous sentiment as one enamoured, if the majesty of goodness were reverenced: would not such a principle serve me by way of police at least as well as a Connecticut Sunday?

—JOURNAL, 1834

Can there be religion without a church? Is there a difference between religion and the forms of religion?

JANUARY 25

Morality requires purity, but purity is not it; requires justice, but justice is not that; requires beneficence, but is something better. Indeed there is a kind of descent and accommodation felt when we leave speaking of Moral Nature to urge a virtue it enjoins. For to the soul in her pure action all the virtues are natural and not painfully acquired. Excite the soul and it becomes suddenly virtuous. Touch the deep heart and all these listless, stingy, beef-eating bystanders will see the dignity of a sentiment, will say, This is good, and all I have I will give for that. Excite the soul, and the weather and the town and your condition in the world all disappear, the world itself loses its solidity, nothing remains but the soul and the Divine Presence in which it lives. Youth and age are indifferent in this presence.

—JOURNAL, 1834

Has your soul ever been excited? If so, did "the weather and the town and your condition in the world all disappear"?

The termination of the world in a man, appears to be the last victory of intelligence. The universal does not attract us until housed in an individual. Who heeds the waste abyss of possibility? The ocean is everywhere the same, but it has no character until seen with the shore or the ship. Who would value any number of miles of Atlantic brine bounded by lines of latitude and longitude? Confine it by granite rocks, let it wash a shore where wise men dwell, and it is filled with expression; and the point of greatest interest is where the land and water meet. So must we admire in man, the form of the formless, the concentration of the vast, the house of reason, the cave of memory. See the play of thoughts! what nimble gigantic creatures are these! what saurians, what palaiotheria shall be named with these agile movers? The great Pan of old, who was clothed in a leopard skin to signify the beautiful variety of things, and the firmament, his coat of stars,—was but the representative of thee, O rich and various Man! thou palace of sight and sound, carrying in thy senses the morning and the night and the unfathomable galaxy; in thy brain, the geometry of the City of God; in thy heart, the bower of love and the realms of right and wrong.

— THE METHOD OF NATURE

How does the universe come to consciousness in you? Do you share Emerson's view of human beings and their destiny?

JANUARY 27

Yesterday night, at fifteen minutes after eight, my little Waldo ended his life.... The sun went up the morning sky with all his light, but the landscape was dishonored by this loss. For this boy, in whose remembrance I have both slept and awaked so oft, decorated for me the morning star, the evening cloud, how much more all the particulars of daily economy; for he had touched with his lively curiosity every trivial fact and circumstance in the household.... For every thing he had his own name and way of thinking, his own pronunciation and manner. And every word came mended from that tongue. A boy of early wisdom, and of a grave and even majestic deportment, of a perfect gentleness. Every tramper that ever tramped is abroad but the little feet are still. He gave up his little innocent breath like a bird.

—JOURNAL, 1842

Can you imagine the grief of losing a child? How would such a loss temper your philosophy of life?

Let man, then, learn the revelation of all nature and all thought to his heart; this, namely; that the Highest dwells within him; that the sources of nature are in his own mind, if the sentiment of duty is there. But if he would know what the great God speaketh, he must "go into his closet and shut the door," as Jesus said. God will not make himself manifest to cowards. He must greatly listen to himself, withdrawing himself from all the accents of other men's devotion. Even their prayers are hurtful to him, until he have made his own. Our religion vulgarly stands on numbers of believers. Whenever the appeal is made—no matter how indirectly—to numbers, proclamation is then and there made, that religion is not. He that finds God a sweet enveloping thought to him never counts his company.... It makes no difference whether the appeal is to numbers or to one. The faith that stands on authority is not faith. The reliance on authority measures the decline of religion, the withdrawal of the soul.

— THE OVER-SOUL

Do you believe that "the Highest dwells within"? Are you convinced by an appeal to numbers? Can a religion with a billion adherents be wrong?

JANUARY 29

To the intelligent, nature converts itself into a vast promise, and will not be rashly explained. Her secret is untold. Many and many an Oedipus arrives: he has the whole mystery teeming in his brain. Alas! the same sorcery has spoiled his skill; no syllable can he shape on his lips. Her mighty orbit vaults like the fresh rainbow into the deep, but no archangel's wing was yet strong enough to follow it, and report of the return of the curve. But it also appears, that our actions are seconded and disposed to greater conclusions than we designed. We are escorted on every hand through life by spiritual agents, and a beneficent purpose lies in wait for us. We cannot bandy words with nature, or deal with her as we deal with persons. If we measure our individual forces against hers, we may easily feel as if we were the sport of an insuperable destiny. But if, instead of identifying ourselves with the work, we feel that the soul of the workman streams through us, we shall find the peace of the morning dwelling first in our hearts, and the fathomless powers of gravity and chemistry, and, over them, of life, preexisting within us in their highest form.

—NATURE

Is there a providence in nature? Have you ever felt escorted by "spiritual agents"?

We are in transition, from the worship of the fathers which enshrined the law in a private and personal history, to a worship which recognizes the true eternity of the law, its presence to you and me, its equal energy in what is called brute nature as in what is called sacred. The next age will behold God in the ethical laws—as mankind begins to see them in this age, self-equal, self-executing, instantaneous and self-affirmed; needing no voucher, no prophet and no miracle besides their own irresistibility,—and will regard natural history, private fortunes and politics, not for themselves, as we have done, but as illustrations of those laws, of that beatitude and love. Nature is too thin a screen; the glory of the One breaks in everywhere.

—THE PREACHER

Do you behold God in ethical laws? Do you see those laws illustrated in natural history and human affairs?

JANUARY 31

I hate this shallow Americanism which hopes to get rich by credit, to get knowledge by raps on midnight tables, to learn the economy of the mind by phrenology, or skill without study, or mastery without apprenticeship, or the sale of goods through pretending that they sell, or power through making believe you are powerful, or through a packed jury or caucus, bribery and "repeating" votes, or wealth by fraud. They think they have got it, but they have got something else,—a crime which calls for another crime, and another devil behind that; these are steps to suicide, infamy and the harming of mankind. We countenance each other in this life of show, puffing, advertisement and manufacture of public opinion; and excellence is lost sight of in the hunger for sudden performance and praise.

—SUCCESS

Do you find a similar shallowness in American society today? What role does the "hunger for sudden performance and praise" play in your life?

FEBRUARY

Meditations

FEBRUARY 1

The good of going into the mountains is that life is reconsidered; it is far from the slavery of your own modes of living and you have opportunity of viewing the town at such a distance as may afford you a just view, nor can you have any such mistaken apprehension as might be expected from the place you occupy and the round of customs you run at home. He who believes in inspiration will come here to seek it. He who believes in the wood-loving muses must woo them here. And he who believes in the reality of his soul will therein find inspiration and muses and God and will come out here to undress himself of pedantry and judge righteous judgment and worship the First Cause.

—JOURNAL, 1832

Where are you "far from the slavery of your own modes of living"? Do you find yourself closer to your soul there?

He has seen but half the universe who never has been shown the House of Pain. As the salt sea covers more than two thirds of the surface of the globe, so sorrow encroaches in man on felicity. The conversation of men is a mixture of regrets and apprehensions. I do not know but the prevalent hue of things to the eye of leisure is melancholy. In the dark hours, our existence seems to be a defensive war, a struggle against the encroaching All, which threatens surely to engulf us soon, and is impatient of our short reprieve. How slender the possession that yet remains to us; how faint the animation! How the spirit seems already to contract its domain, retiring within narrower walls by the loss of memory, leaving its planted fields to erasure and annihilation. Already our own thoughts and words have an alien sound. There is a simultaneous diminution of memory and hope. Projects that once we laughed and leaped to execute, find us, now sleepy and preparing to lie down in the snow. And in the serene hours we have no courage to spare. We cannot afford to let go any advantages. The riches of body or mind which we do not need today, are the reserved fund against the calamity that may arrive tomorrow.

— THE TRAGIC

Does your philosophy of life contain an element of the tragic? How can you store up "riches of body and mind" to use if needed in the future?

Shall I say, then, that, as far as we can trace the natural history of the soul, its health consists in the fullness of its reception,— call it piety, call it veneration—in the fact, that enthusiasm is organized therein. What is best in any work of art, but that part which the work itself seems to require and do; that which the man cannot do again, that which flows from the hour and the occasion, like the eloquence of men in a tumultuous debate?... This ecstatical state seems to direct a regard to the whole and not to the parts; to the cause and not to the ends; to the tendency, and not to the act. It respects genius and not talent; hope, and not possession; the anticipation of all things by the intellect, and not the history itself; art, and not works of art; poetry, and not experiment; virtue, and not duties. There is no office or function of man but is rightly discharged by this divine method, and nothing that is not noxious to him if detached from its universal relations.

—THE METHOD OF NATURE

Do you ever find yourself in an ecstatic state, a condition of flow, when you feel in accord with the "divine method"? What would it mean to apply this divine method to all of your activities?

FEBRUARY 4

And now at last the highest truth on this subject remains unsaid; probably cannot be said; for all that we say is the far-off remembering of the intuition. That thought, by what I can now nearest approach to say it, is this. When good is near you, when you have life in yourself, it is not by any known or accustomed way; you shall not discern the footprints of any other; you shall not see the face of man; you shall not hear any name,—the way, the thought, the good, shall be wholly strange and new.... In the hour of vision, there is nothing that can be called gratitude, nor properly joy. The soul raised over passion beholds identity and eternal causation, perceives the self-existence of Truth and Right, and calms itself with knowing that all things go well. Vast spaces of nature, the Atlantic Ocean, the South Sea,—long intervals of time, years, centuries,—are of no account. This which I think and feel underlay every former state of life and circumstances, as it does underlie my present, and what is called life, and what is called death.

—Self-Reliance

Have you ever intuited something that seemed beyond the usual categories of experience? Have you had the sense that "all things go well"?

FEBRUARY 5

The soul gives itself, alone, original, and pure, to the Lonely, Original, and Pure, who, on that condition, gladly inhabits, leads, and speaks through it. Then it is glad, young, and nimble. It is not wise, but it sees through all things. It is not called religious, but it is innocent. It calls the light its own, and feels that the grass grows and the stone falls by a law inferior to, and dependent on, its nature. Behold, it saith, I am born into the great, the universal mind. I, the imperfect, adore my own Perfect. I am somehow receptive of the great soul, and thereby I do overlook the sun and the stars, and feel them to be the fair accidents and effects which change and pass. More and more the surges of everlasting nature enter into me, and I become public and human in my regards and actions. So come I to live in thoughts, and act with energies, which are immortal. Thus revering the soul, ... man will come to see that the world is the perennial miracle which the soul worketh, and be less astonished at particular wonders; he will learn that there is no profane history; that all history is sacred; that the universe is represented in an atom, in a moment of time. He will weave no longer a spotted life of shreds and patches, but he will live with a divine unity.

—THE OVER-SOUL

When "the surges of everlasting nature" enter into you, do you become a more universal person? Do you aspire to "live life with a divine unity"?

FEBRUARY 6

All over the wide fields of earth grows the prunella or self-heal. After every foolish day we sleep off the fumes and furies of its hours; and though we are always engaged with particulars, and often enslaved to them, we bring with us to every experiment the innate universal laws. These, while they exist in the mind as ideas, stand around us in nature forever embodied, a present sanity to expose and cure the insanity of men. Our servitude to particulars betrays into a hundred foolish expectations. We anticipate a new era from the invention of a locomotive, or a balloon; the new engine brings with it the old checks. They say that by electro-magnetism, your salad shall be grown from the seed, whilst your fowl is roasting for dinner: it is a symbol of our modern aims and endeavors,—of our condensation and acceleration of objects: but nothing is gained: nature cannot be cheated: man's life is but seventy salads long, grow they swift or grow they slow. In these checks and impossibilities, however, we find our advantage, not less than in the impulses. Let the victory fall where it will, we are on that side. And the knowledge that we traverse the whole scale of being, from the center to the poles of nature, and have some stake in every possibility, lends that sublime lustre to death, which philosophy and religion have too outwardly and literally striven to express in the popular doctrine of the immortality of the soul. The reality is more excellent than the report. Here is no ruin, no discontinuity, no spent ball. The divine circulations never rest nor linger.

—Nature

Do you "have some stake in every possibility"? How do you define immortality?

FEBRUARY 7

The health and welfare of man consists in ascent from surfaces to solids; from occupation with details to knowledge of the design; from self-activity of talents, which lose their way by the lust of display, to the controlling and reinforcing of talents by the emanation of character. All that we call religion, all that saints and churches and Bibles from the beginning of the world have aimed at, is to suppress this impertinent surface-action, and animate man to central and entire action. The human race are afflicted with a St. Vitus's dance; their fingers and toes, their members, their senses, their talents, are superfluously active, while the torpid heart gives no oracle. When that wakes, it will revolutionize the world. Let that speak, and all these rebels will fly to their loyalty. Now every man defeats his own action,—professes this but practices the reverse; with one hand rows, and with the other backs water. A man acts not from one motive, but from many shifting fears and short motives; it is as if he were ten or twenty less men than himself, acting at discord with one another, so that the result of most lives is zero. But when he shall act from one motive, and all his faculties play true, it is clear mathematically, is it not, that this will tell in the result as if twenty men had cooperated,—will give new senses, new wisdom of its own kind; that is, not more facts, nor new combinations, but divination, or direct intuition of men and things?

—THE PREACHER

Do you feel at cross-purposes in your own life? Do you live at a superficial level?

[The] illusion haunts us, that a long duration, as a year, a decade, a century, is valuable. But an old French sentence says, "God works in moments".... We ask for long life, but 'tis deep life, or grand moments, that signify. Let the measure of time be spiritual, not mechanical. Life is unnecessarily long. Moments of insight, of fine personal relation, a smile, a glance,—what ample borrowers of eternity they are! Life culminates and concentrates; and Homer said, "The gods ever give to mortals their apportioned share of reason only on one day."

— WORKS AND DAYS

How do you measure time? Have you experienced moments that were "borrowers of eternity"?

There are all degrees of proficiency in knowledge of the world. It is sufficient, to our present purpose, to indicate three. One class live to the utility of the symbol; esteeming health and wealth a final good. Another class live above this mark to the beauty of the symbol; as the poet, and artist, and the naturalist, and man of science. A third class live above the beauty of the symbol to the beauty of the thing signified; these are wise men. The first class have common sense; the second, taste; and the third, spiritual perception. Once in a long time, a man traverses the whole scale, and sees and enjoys the symbol solidly; then also has a clear eye for its beauty, and, lastly, whilst he pitches his tent on this sacred volcanic isle of nature, does not offer to build houses and barns thereon, reverencing the splendor of the God which he sees bursting through each chink and cranny.

— PRUDENCE

Do you see yourself on any of these three levels of proficiency? How do you move from one level to another?

Do your thing: let your expense be for what is proper to you. Let your genius spend to the uttermost. Every man's expense and economy must proceed from his character. A carpenter cannot be a carpenter without his tools, which he must buy, cost what they may; or the engineer, without his theodolite and chain; or the painter, without easel, and pigments, and canvas; or the astronomer, without azimuth and telescope, a farmer without lands, or a manufacturer without mills, not the scholar without books. As long as your genius buys, the investment is safe. And great trust must be given to that impulse. For pleasure, buy not; for the eyes of others, buy not; for the chances of gain (unless you are a merchant), buy not; but for the work to which you are born, and which you intermit not, night or day, spend like a monarch. To save, on this particular point, is not economy, but suicide. For, economy does not consist in saving coals or candles, but, in turning the time while they burn into life. One thing is certain, you cannot afford to be a fool. Spend here, for the economy of economies is to put reality into your expense, to do your work, to put reality into the world. A seaman will not economize by buying rotten rope or rotten canvas if he is to go in the ship. Do your thing, and spend for your expense.

—Economy

What do you spend on? How do you decide what is spending for genius and what is spending for show?

Jesus Christ belonged to the true race of prophets. He saw with open eye the mystery of the soul. Drawn by its severe harmony, ravished with its beauty, he lived in it, and had his being there. Alone in all history, he estimated the greatness of man. One man was true to what is in you and me. He saw that God incarnates himself in man, and evermore goes forth anew to take possession of his world. He said, in this jubilee of sublime emotion, "I am divine. Through me, God acts; through me, speaks. Would you see God, see me; or, see thee, when thou also thinkest as I now think." But what a distortion did his doctrine and memory suffer in the same, in the next, and the following ages! There is no doctrine of the Reason which will bear to be taught by the Understanding. The understanding caught this high chant from the poet's lips, and said, in the next age, "This was Jehovah come down out of heaven. I will kill you, if you say he was a man." The idioms of his language, and the figures of his rhetoric, have usurped the place of his truth; and churches are not built on his principles, but on his tropes. Christianity became a Mythus, as the poetic teaching of Greece and of Egypt, before. He spoke of miracles; for he felt that man's life was a miracle, and all that man doth, and he knew that this daily miracle shines, as the character ascends. But the word Miracle, as pronounced by Christian churches, gives a false impression; it is Monster. It is not one with the blowing clover and the falling rain.

— THE DIVINITY SCHOOL ADDRESS

What is your view of Christ? Do you believe that Jesus' message has been distorted?

FEBRUARY 12

Always pay; for, first or last, you must pay your entire debt. Persons and events may stand for a time between you and justice, but it is only a postponement. You must pay at last your own debt. If you are wise, you will dread a prosperity which only loads you with more. Benefit is the end of nature. But for every benefit which you receive, a tax is levied. He is great who confers the most benefits. He is base—and that is the one base thing in the universe—to receive favors and render none. In the order of nature we cannot render benefits to those from whom we receive them, or only seldom. But the benefit we receive must be rendered again, line for line, deed for deed, cent for cent, to somebody. Beware of too much good staying in your hand. It will fast corrupt and worm worms. Pay it away quickly in some sort.

—Compensation

What does it mean to "pay at last your own debt"? Have you paid yours?

The growth of the intellect is spontaneous in every expansion. The mind that grows could not predict the times, the means, the mode of that spontaneity. God enters by a private door into every individual. Long prior to the age of reflection is the thinking of the mind. Out of darkness, it came insensibly into the marvellous light of today. In the period of infancy it accepted and disposed of all impressions from the surrounding creation after its own way. Whatever any mind doth or saith is after a law; and this native law remains over it after it has come to reflection or conscious thought. In the most worn, pedantic, introverted self-tormentor's life, the greatest part is incalculable by him, unforeseen, unimaginable, and must be, until he can take himself up by his own ears. What am I? What has my will done to make me that I am? Nothing. I have been floated into this thought, this hour, this connection of events, by secret currents of might and mind, and my ingenuity and willfulness have not thwarted, have not aided to an appreciable degree.

—INTELLECT

Are your own best thoughts spontaneous? Do you ever feel that "secret currents of might and mind" have brought you to certain conclusions about the meaning of life?

FEBRUARY 14

Thus we trace Fate, in matter, mind, and morals,—in race, in retardations of strata, and in thought and character as well. It is everywhere bound or limitation. But Fate has its lord; limitation its limits; is different seen from above and from below; from within and from without. For, though Fate is immense, so is power, which is the other fact in the dual world, immense. If Fate follows and limits power, power attends and antagonizes Fate. We must respect Fate as natural history, but there is more than natural history.... Man is not order of nature, sack and sack, belly and members, link in a chain, nor any ignominious baggage, but a stupendous antagonism, a dragging together of the poles of the Universe. He betrays his relation to what is below him, ... and has paid for the new powers by loss of some of the old ones. But the lightning which explodes and fashions planets, maker of planets and suns, is in him. On one side, elemental order, sandstone and granite, rock-ledges, peat-bog, forest, sea and shore; and, on the other part, thought, the spirit which composes and decomposes nature,—here they are, side by side, god and devil, mind and matter, king and conspirator, belt and spasm, riding peacefully together in the eye and brain of every man.

—FATE

Do you have power over your fate? Are you able to accept things you can't change?

FEBRUARY 15

At certain happy hours, each man is conscious of a secret heaven within him, a realm of undiscovered sciences, or slumbering powers; a heaven, of which these feats of talent, are no measure; it arches like a sky, over all that it has done, or that has been done, and suggests unfathomable power. All that is urged by the saint, for the superiority of faith over works, is as truly urged for the highest state of intellectual perception or beholding, over any intellectual performance, as the creation of algebra, or of the *Iliad*. Sometimes under the spell of poetry, sometimes in solitude, sometimes in deep conversation on moral problems, we come out of our egg-shell existence into the great Dome, and see the Zenith over us, and the Nadir under us.

—Powers of the Mind

When was the last time you were conscious of "a secret heaven within"? What brings you out of your own "egg-shell existence" to a consciousness of "unfathomable power"?

FEBRUARY 16

Each man has an aptitude born with him. Do your work.... Yet whilst this self-truth is essential to the exhibition of the world and to the growth and glory of each mind, it is rare to find a man who believes his own thought or who speaks that which he was created to say.... We do not believe our own thought; we must serve somebody; we must quote somebody; we dote on the old and distant; we are tickled by great names; we import the religion of other nations; we quote their opinions; we cite their laws.... Self-trust is the first secret of success, the belief that if you are here the authorities of the universe put you here, and for cause, or with some task strictly appointed you in your constitution, and so long as you work at that you are well and successful.

—SUCCESS

Do you trust your own thought, or do you quote the opinions of others? Do you believe that "the authorities of the universe put you here" for a purpose?

FEBRUARY 17

The finite is the foam of the infinite. We stand on the shore and see the froth and shells which the sea has thrown up, and we call the sea by the name of that boundary, as, the German Ocean,—the English channel,—the Mediterranean Sea. We do the like with the Soul. We see the world which it once has made, and we call that God, though it was only one moment's production, and there have been a thousand moments and a thousand productions since. But we are to learn to transfer our view to the Sea instead of the Shore, the living sea instead of the changing shore, to the energy instead of the limitation, to the Creator instead of the World. We must ever tend to a good life.

—JOURNAL, 1839

Are you able to view the sea rather than the shore? How difficult is it to do so?

There are two theories of life; one for the demonstration of our talent, the other for the education of the man. One is activity, the busybody, the following of that practical talent which we have, in the belief that what is so natural, easy and pleasant to us and desirable to others will surely lead us out safely; in this direction lie usefulness, comfort, society, low power of all sorts. The other is trust, religion, consent to be nothing for eternity, entranced waiting, the worship of ideas. This is solitary, grand, secular. They are in perpetual balance and strife. One is talent, the other genius. One is skill, the other character. We are continually tempted to sacrifice genius to talent, the hope and promise of insight to the lust of a freer demonstration of those gifts we have; and we buy this freedom to glitter by the loss of general health.... Wide is the gulf between genius and talent.

—NATURAL HISTORY OF INTELLECT

Have you sacrificed genius for talent in your life? How might you give a freer demonstration of your genius?

FEBRUARY 19

I ask not for the great, the remote, the romantic; what is doing in Italy or Arabia; what is Greek art, or Provencal minstrelsy; I embrace the common, I explore and sit at the feet of the familiar, the low. Give me insight into today, and you may have the antique and future worlds. What would we really know the meaning of? The meal in the firkin; the milk in the pan; the ballad in the street; the news of the boat; the glance of the eye; the form and the gait of the body;—show me the ultimate reason of these matters; show me the sublime presence of the highest spiritual cause lurking, as always it does lurk, in these suburbs and extremities of nature; let me see every trifle bristling with the polarity that ranges it instantly on an eternal law; and the shop, the plough, and the ledger, referred to the like cause by which light undulates and poets sing;—and the world lies no longer a dull miscellany and lumber-room, but has form and order; there is no trifle; there is no puzzle; but one design unites and animates the farthest pinnacle and the lowest trench.

—THE AMERICAN SCHOLAR

Do you embrace the common? Do you practice a spirituality of everyday life?

A little consideration of what takes place around us every day would show us, that a higher law than that of our will regulates events; that our painful labors are unnecessary, and fruitless; that only in our easy, simple, spontaneous action are we strong, and by contenting ourselves with obedience we become divine. Belief and love,—a believing love will relieve us of a vast load of care. O my brothers, God exists. There is a soul at the centre of nature, and over the will of every man, so that none of us can wrong the universe. It has so infused its strong enchantment into nature, that we prosper when we accept its advice, and when we struggle to wound its creatures, our hands are glued to our sides, or they beat our own breasts. The whole course of things goes to teach us faith. We need only obey. There is guidance for each of us, and by lowly listening we shall hear the right word. Why need you choose so painfully your place, and occupation, and associates, and modes of action, and of entertainment? Certainly there is a possible right for you that precludes the need of balance and wilful election. For you there is a reality, a fit place and congenial duties. Place yourself in the middle of the stream of power and wisdom which animates all whom it floats, and you are without effort impelled to truth, to right, and a perfect contentment. Then you put all gainsayers in the wrong. Then you are the world, the measure of right, of truth, of beauty.

— SPIRITUAL LAWS

Do you think "a higher law than that of our will regulates events"? Do you think "none of us can wrong the universe"?

FEBRUARY 21

Objections and criticism we have had our fill of. There are objections to every course of life and action, and the practical wisdom infers an indifferency, from the omnipresence of objection. The whole frame of things preaches indifferency. Do not craze yourself with thinking, but go about your business anywhere. Life is not intellectual or critical, but sturdy. Its chief good is for well-mixed people who can enjoy what they find, without question.... To fill the hour,—that is happiness; to fill the hour, and leave no crevice for a repentance or an approval. We live amid surfaces, and the true art of life is to skate well on them. Under the oldest mouldiest conventions, a man of native force prospers just as well as in the newest world, and that by skill of handling and treatment.

— EXPERIENCE

How well have you managed to "fill the hour"? Can you enjoy what you find, without question?

The whole state of man is a state of culture; and its flowering and completion may be described as Religion, or Worship. There is always some religion, some hope and fear extended into the invisible,—from the blind boding which nails a horseshoe to the mast or the threshold, up to the song of the Elders in the Apocalypse. But the religion cannot rise above the state of the votary. Heaven always bears some proportion to earth. The god of the cannibals will be a cannibal, of the crusaders a crusader, and of the merchants a merchant. In all ages, souls out of time, extraordinary, prophetic, are born, who are rather related to the system of the world, than to their particular age and locality. These announce absolute truths, which, with whatever reverence received, are speedily dragged down into a savage interpretation.

— WORSHIP

Is your behavior a reflection of your religion, or is your religion a reflection of your behavior? How is religion improved if it cannot "rise above the votary"?

Whilst the man of ideas converses with truths as thoughts, they exist also as plastic forces, as the soul of a man, the soul of a plant, the genius or constitution of any part of nature, which makes it what it is. Like a fragment of ice in the sea, so man exists in the firmament of truth which made him. He is a thought embodied, and the world of thought exists around him for element. The thought which was in the world, part and parcel of the world, has disengaged itself, and taken an independent existence. But of those elemental organic thoughts which we involuntarily express in the mould of our features, in the tendency of our characters, there is no measure known to us. The institution draws all its solidity and impressiveness from the virulence and centrality of the thought. The history of the world is nothing but the procession of clothed ideas.

—THE POWERS AND LAWS OF THOUGHT

Do you consider yourself as "part and parcel of the world" or as separate from it? What difference does it make?

FEBRUARY 24

Is it not all in us, how strangely! Look at this congregation of men; ... the words might be said that would make them stagger and reel like a drunken man. Who doubts it? Were you ever instructed by a wise and eloquent man? Remember then. Were not the words that made your blood run cold, that brought the blood to your cheeks, that made you tremble or delighted you, did they not sound to you as old as yourself? Was it not truth that you knew before or do you ever expect to be moved from the pulpit or from man by any thing but plain truth? Never. It is God in you that responds to God without or affirms his own words trembling on the lips of another.

—JOURNAL, 1831

Were you ever instructed by "a wise and eloquent" minister? Have you ever thought you already knew the truth of what was preached from the pulpit?

In short there ought to be no such thing as Fate. As long as we use this word, it is a sign of our impotence and that we are not yet ourselves. There is now a sublime revelation in each of us which makes us so strangely aware and certain of our riches that although I have never since I was born for so much as one moment expressed the truth, and although I have never heard the expression of it from any other, I know that the whole is here—the wealth of the universe is for me. Everything is explicable and practicable for me. And yet whilst I adore this ineffable life which is at my heart, it will not condescend to gossip with me, it will not announce to me any particulars of science, it will not enter into the details of my biography, and say to me why I have a son and daughters born to me, or why my son dies in his sixth year of joy. Herein I have this latent omniscience coexistent with omniignorance. Moreover, whilst this Deity glows at the heart, and by his unlimited presentments gives me all power, I know that tomorrow will be as this day, I am a dwarf, and I remain a dwarf. That is to say, I believe in Fate. As long as I am weak, I shall talk of Fate; whenever God fills me with his fullness, I shall see the disappearance of Fate. I am *Defeated* all the time; yet to Victory I am born.

—JOURNAL, 1842

Are you hemmed in by fate? Are you born to victory?

We are driven by instinct to hive innumerable experiences which are of no visible value, and we may revolve through many lives before we shall assimilate or exhaust them. Now there is nothing in Nature capricious, or whimsical, or accidental, or unsupported. Nature never moves by jumps, but always in steady and supported advances. The implanting of a desire indicates that the gratification of that desire is in the constitution of the creature that feels it; the wish for food, the wish for motion, the wish for sleep, for society, for knowledge, are not random whims, but grounded in the structure of the creature, and meant to be satisfied by food, by motion, by sleep, by society, by knowledge. If there is the desire to live, and in larger sphere, with more knowledge and power, it is because life and knowledge and power are good for us, and we are the natural depositories of these gifts. The love of life is out of all proportion to the value set on a single day, and seems to indicate, like all our other experiences, a conviction of immense resources and possibilities proper to us, on which we have never drawn.

—IMMORTALITY

Do you desire to live "in larger sphere"? What does this mean to you?

There is no chance, and no anarchy, in the universe. All is system and gradation. Every god is there sitting in his sphere. The young mortal enters the hall of the firmament: there is he alone with them alone, they pouring on him benedictions and gifts, and beckoning him up to their thrones. On the instant, and incessantly, fall snow-storms of illusions. He fancies himself in a vast crowd which sways this way and that, and whose movement and doings he must obey: he fancies himself poor, orphaned, insignificant. The mad crowd drives hither and thither, now furiously commanding this thing to be done, now that. What is he that he should resist their will, and think or act for himself? Every moment, new changes, and new showers of deceptions, to baffle and distract him. And when, by and by, for an instant, the air clears, and the cloud lifts a little, there are the gods still sitting around him on their thrones,—they alone with him alone.

—Illusions

Do you agree with Emerson that "there is no chance, and no anarchy, in the universe"? Have you ever found yourself in the throne room of the gods?

FEBRUARY 28

The Supreme Critic on the errors of the past and the present, and the only prophet of that which must be, is that great nature in which we rest, as the earth lies in the soft arms of the atmosphere; that Unity, that Over-soul, within which every man's particular being is contained and made one with all other; that common heart, of which all sincere conversation is the worship, to which all right action is submission; that overpowering reality which confutes our tricks and talents, and constrains every one to pass for what he is, and to speak from his character, and not from his tongue, and which evermore tends to pass into our thought and hand, and become wisdom, and virtue, and power, and beauty. We live in succession, in division, in parts, in particles. Meantime within man is the soul of the whole; the wise silence; the universal beauty, to which every part and particle is equally related; the eternal ONE. And this deep power in which we exist, and whose beatitude is all accessible to us, is not only self-sufficing and perfect in every hour, but the act of seeing and the thing seen, the seer and the spectacle, the subject and the object, are one. We see the world piece by piece, as the sun, the moon, the animal, the tree; but the whole, of which these are the shining parts, is the soul.

—THE OVER-SOUL

Do you believe in a unity, an over-soul, within which all things exist? How would you describe it?

MARCH

Meditations

MARCH 1

We have had many harbingers and forerunners; but of a purely spiritual life, history has afforded no example. I mean, we have yet no man who has leaned entirely on his character, and eaten angels' food; who, trusting to his sentiments, found life made of miracles; who, working for universal aims, found himself fed, he knew not how; clothed, sheltered, and weaponed, he knew not how, and yet it was done by his own hands. Only in the instinct of the lower animals, we find the suggestion of the methods of it, and something higher than our understanding. The squirrel hoards nuts, and the bee gathers honey, without knowing what they do, and they are thus provided for without selfishness or disgrace.

—THE TRANSCENDENTALIST

Can you think of any such "harbingers and forerunners"? Is it quite impossible to subsist only on "angels' food"?

The whole secret of a teacher's force lies in the conviction that men are convertible. And they are. They want awakening. Get the soul out of bed, out of her deep habitual sleep, out into God's universe, to a perception of its beauty and hearing of its Call and your vulgar man, your prosy selfish sensualist awakes, a God, and is conscious of force to shake the world....Spend the Sunday morning well and the hours shall shine with immortal light, shall epitomize history, shall sing heavenly psalms. Your way to church shall be short as the way to the playground is to a child, and something holy and wise shall sit upon all the countenances there and shall inspire the preacher's words with a wisdom not their own. Spend the Sunday morning ill, and you will hardly hear a good sermon anywhere. Could it be made apparent, what is really true, that the whole future is in the bottom of the heart, that, in proportion as your life is spent within,—in that measure are you invulnerable? In proportion as you penetrate facts for the law, and events for the cause, in that measure is your knowledge real, your condition generally conformed to a stable idea, and the future foreseen.

—JOURNAL, 1834

Do you ever feel that your soul is habitually asleep? What can you do to wake it up? Have you spent a Sunday morning well recently?

Men and women at thirty years, and even earlier, have lost all spring and vivacity, and if they fail in their first enterprises, they throw up the game. But whether we, and those who are next to us, are more or less vulnerable, no theory of life can have any right, which leaves out of account the values of vice, pain, disease, poverty, insecurity, disunion, fear, and death. What are the conspicuous tragic elements in human nature? The bitterest tragic element in life to be derived from an intellectual source is the belief in a brute Fate or Destiny; the belief that the order of nature and events is controlled by a law not adapted to man, nor man to that, but which holds on its way to the end, serving him if his wishes chance to lie in the same course,—crushing him if his wishes lie contrary to it,—and heedless whether it serves or crushes him.

— THE TRAGIC

How does your philosophy of life account for suffering and pain? Is suffering merely random, or is there an element of fate or destiny involved?

An individual man is a fruit which it cost all the foregoing ages to form and ripen. The history of the genesis or the old mythology repeats itself in the experience of every child. He too is a demon or god thrown into a particular chaos, where he strives ever to lead things from disorder into order. Each individual soul is such, in virtue of its being a power to translate the world into some particular language of its own; if not into a picture, a statue, or a dance,—why, then, into a trade, an art, a science, a mode of living, a conversation, a character, an influence. . . . When Nature has work to be done, she creates a genius to do it.

— THE METHOD OF NATURE

How, in your vocation, have you been able to translate the world into some particular language? What language does your soul speak?

MARCH 5

Life only avails, not the having lived. Power ceases in the instant of repose; it resides in the moment of transition from a past to a new state, in the shooting of the gulf, in the darting to an aim. This one fact the world hates, that the soul *becomes*; for that for ever degrades the past, turns all riches to poverty, all reputation to a shame, confounds the saint with the rogue, shoves Jesus and Judas equally aside. Why, then, do we prate of self-reliance? Inasmuch as the soul is present there will be power not confident but agent. To talk of reliance is a poor external way of speaking. Speak rather of that which relies, because it works and is.

—SELF-RELIANCE

Do you find exhilaration and energy in "the shooting of the gulf," in the transition from one state of being to another? What does "the soul becomes" mean?

MARCH 6

The eye is the first circle; the horizon which it forms is the second; and throughout nature this primary figure is repeated without end. It is the highest emblem in the cipher of the world. St. Augustine described the nature of God as a circle whose centre was everywhere, and its circumference nowhere. We are all our lifetime reading the copious sense of this first of forms. One moral we have already deduced, in considering the circular or compensatory character of every human action. Another analogy we shall now trace; that every action admits of being outdone. Our life is an apprenticeship to the truth, that around every circle another can be drawn; that there is no end in nature, but every end is a beginning; that there is always another dawn risen on mid-noon, and under every deep a lower deep opens. This fact, as far as it symbolizes the moral fact of the Unattainable, the flying Perfect, around which the hands of man can never meet, at once the inspirer and the condemner of every success, may conveniently serve us to connect many illustrations of human power in every department.

— CIRCLES

How does a circle symbolize spiritual growth? What other symbols are meaningful to you?

MARCH 7

Prayer is the contemplation of the facts of life from the highest point of view. It is the soliloquy of a beholding and jubilant soul. It is the spirit of God pronouncing his works good. But prayer as a means to effect a private end is meanness and theft. It supposes dualism and not unity in nature and consciousness. As soon as the man is at one with God, he will not beg. He will then see prayer in all action. The prayer of the farmer kneeling in his field to weed it, the prayer of the rower kneeling with the stroke of his oar, are true prayers heard throughout nature, though for cheap ends.

—SELF-RELIANCE

What is your definition of prayer? Do you pray? How and what for?

MARCH 8

The lessons of the moral sentiment are, once for all, an eman-
cipation from that anxiety which takes the joy out of all life. It
teaches a great peace. It comes itself from the highest place. It
is that, which being in all sound natures, and strongest in the
best and most gifted men, we know to be implanted by the
Creator of Men. It is a commandment at every moment and in
every condition of life to do the duty of that moment and the
abstain from doing the wrong. And it is so near and inward and
constitutional to each, that no commandment can compare
with it in authority. All wise men regard it as the voice of the
Creator himself.

—The Preacher

---

*Where does your own conscience come from? Do you consider
it a reliable moral guide?*

Think me not unkind and rude,
    That I walk alone in wood and glen;
I go to the god of the wood
    To fetch his word to men.

Tax not my sloth that I
    Fold my arms beside the brook;
Each cloud that floated in the sky
    Writes a letter in my book.

Chide me not, laborious band,
    For the idle flowers I brought;
Every aster in my hand
    Goes home loaded with a thought.

There was never mystery,
    But 'tis figured in the flowers,
Was never secret history,
    But birds tell it in the bowers.

One harvest from thy field
    Homeward brought the oxen strong;
A second crop thine acres yield,
    Which I gather in a song.

— THE APOLOGY

What word have you fetched from the god of the wood? Do you feel apologetic for the time you spend in nature?

MARCH 10

Who shall define to me an Individual? I behold with awe and delight many illustrations of the One Universal Mind. I see my being imbedded in it. As a plant in the earth so I grow in God. I am only a form of God. God is the soul of Me. I can even with a mountainous aspiring say, *I am God*, by transferring my *Me* out of the flimsy and unclean precincts of my body, my fortunes, my private will, and meekly retiring upon the holy austerities of the Just and the Loving—upon the secret fountains of Nature. That thin and difficult ether, I also can breathe. The mortal lungs and nostrils burst and shrivel, but the soul itself needeth no organs; it is all element and all organ. Yet why not always so?

—JOURNAL, 1837

Have you ever felt imbedded in "the One Universal Mind"? What difference does that make to you?

My belief in the use of a course on philosophy is that the student shall learn to appreciate the miracle of the mind; shall learn its subtle but immense power, or shall begin to learn it; shall come to know that in seeing and in no tradition he must find what truth is; that he shall see in it the source of all traditions, and shall see each one of them as better or worse statement of its revelations; shall come to trust it entirely, as the only true; shall cleave to God against the name of God. When he has once known the oracle he will need no priest. And if he finds at first with some alarm how impossible it is to accept many things which the hot or mild sectarian may insist on his believing, he will be armed by his insight and brave to meet all inconvenience and all resistance it may cost him.

—NATURAL HISTORY OF THE INTELLECT

Do you judge the truth of traditions by your own experience? Is this your definition of philosophy?

MARCH 12

The spirit only can teach. Not any profane man, not any sensual, not any liar, not any slave can teach, but only he can give, who has; he only can create, who is. The man on whom the soul descends, through whom the soul speaks, alone can teach. Courage, piety, love, wisdom, can teach; and every man can open his door to these angels, and they shall bring him the gift of tongues. But the man who aims to speak as books enable, as synods use, as the fashion guides, and as interest commands, babbles. Let him hush.

—THE DIVINITY SCHOOL ADDRESS

Have you had any teachers through whom the soul spoke?

Human labor, through all its forms, from the sharpening of a stake to the construction of a city or an epic, is one immense illustration of the perfect compensation of the universe. The absolute balance of Give and Take, the doctrine that every thing has its price,—and if that price is not paid, not that thing but something else is obtained, and that it is impossible to get any thing without its price,—is not less sublime in the columns of a ledger than in the budgets of states, in the laws of light and darkness, in all the action and reaction of nature. I cannot doubt that the high laws which each man sees implicated in those processes with which he is conversant, the stern ethics which sparkle on his chisel-edge, which are measured out by his plumb and foot-rule, which stand as manifest in the footing of the shop-bill as in the history of a state,—do recommend to him his trade, and though seldom named, exalt his business to his imagination.

—COMPENSATION

Do you see "the absolute balance of Give and Take" in your own labor? How does it manifest itself?

MARCH 14

Our spontaneous action is always the best. You cannot with your best deliberation and heed, come so close to any question as your spontaneous glance shall bring you, whilst you rise from your bed, or walk abroad in the morning after meditating the matter before sleep on the previous night. Our thinking is a pious reception. Our truth of thought is therefore vitiated as much by too violent direction given by our will, as by too great negligence. We do not determine what we will think. We only open our senses, clear away, as we can, all obstruction from the fact, and suffer the intellect to see. We have little control over our thoughts. We are the prisoners of ideas. They catch us up for moments into their heaven, and so fully engage us, that we take no thought for the morrow, gaze like children, without an effort to make them our own. By and by we fall out of that rapture, bethink us where we have been, what we have seen, and repeat, as truly as we can, what we have beheld. As far as we can recall these ecstasies, we carry away in the ineffaceable memory the result, and all men and all the ages confirm it. It is called Truth. But the moment we cease to report, and attempt to correct and contrive, it is not truth.

—INTELLECT

Is your best thinking "a pious reception"? Have you been caught up in the rapture of ideas? Was it difficult to recapture them later?

MARCH 15

Let us build altars to the Blessed Unity which holds nature and souls in perfect solution, and compels every atom to serve an universal end. I do not wonder at a snow-flake, a shell, a summer landscape, or the glory of the stars; but at the necessity of beauty under which the universe lies; that all is and must be pictorial; that the rainbow, and the curve of the horizon, and the arch of the blue vault are only results from the organism of the eye. There is no need for foolish amateurs to fetch me to admire a garden of flowers, or a sun-gilt cloud, or a waterfall, when I cannot look without seeing splendor and grace. How idle to choose a random sparkle here or there, when the indwelling necessity plants the rose of beauty on the brow of chaos, and discloses the central intention of Nature to be harmony and joy.

—FATE

Are you able to see "splendor and grace" in everything? Does the beauty we see come from an inner tendency to "harmony and joy"?

MARCH 16

The advance, everlasting. All things flow, said the Ancient; all flows.... The Universe is only in transit, or, we behold it shooting the gulf from past to future: And this the mind shares. Transition is the attitude of power, and the essential act of life. The whole history of the mind is passage, pulsation, dark and light, preparation and arrival; and again, preparation and arrival. And as we only truly possess what we mentally possess, that is, what we understand, we are passing into new earths and new heavens,—into new earths, by chemistry; into new heavens, in fact, by the movement of our solar system, and, in thought, by our better knowledge. The habit of saliency, of not pausing, but going on, is a sort of importation and domestication of the Divine effort into a man.

—THE NATURAL METHOD OF MENTAL PHILOSOPHY

What does the "everlasting advance" mean to you in terms of your own spiritual life? Do you agree with Emerson that in transition is power and "the essential act of life"? Is there anything that is unchanging?

I believe in the perseverance of the saints, I believe in effectual calling, I believe in the Life Everlasting. I am here to represent humanity: it is by no means necessary that I should live, but it is by all means necessary that I should act rightly. If there is danger, I must face it. I tremble; What of that?...How many people are there in Boston? Two hundred thousand. Then there are so many sects. I go for Churches of one. Break no springs; make no cripples. A fatal disservice does this Swedenborg, or other lawyer, who offers to do my thinking for me. Nature, when she sends a new mind into the world, fills it beforehand with a desire for that she wishes it to know and do. The charm of life is this variety of genius, these contrasts and flavors by which Heaven has modulated the identity of truth. And there is a perpetual hankering among people to violate this individuality,—to warp his ways of thinking and behaviour to resemble or reflect their thinking and behavior. And I suffer whenever I see that common sight of a parent or senior imposing his opinion and way of thinking and being on a young soul to which it is totally unfit.

—ESSENTIAL PRINCIPLES OF RELIGION

Are you a member of "a church of one"? Do you see "a perpetual hankering among people to violate" individuality? Have you felt violated in this way yourself?

MARCH 18

We remember when in early youth the earth spoke and the heavens glowed; when an evening, any evening, grim and wintry, sleet and snow, was enough for us; the houses were in the air. Now it costs a rare combination of clouds and lights to overcome the common and mean. What is it we look for in the landscape, in sunsets and sunrises, in the sea and the firmament? What but a compensation for the cramp and pettiness of human performances? We bask in the day, and the mind finds somewhat as great as itself.

—Success

Do you have memories of your youth when "the earth spoke and the heavens glowed"? Where do you find "a compensation for the cramp and pettiness of human performances"?

MARCH 19

Day creeps after day each full of facts—dull, strange, despised things that we cannot enough despise,—call heavy, prosaic, desart. And presently the aroused intellect finds gold and gems in one of these scorned facts, then finds that the day of facts is a rock of diamonds, that a fact is an Epiphany of God, that on every fact of his life he should rear a temple of wonder, joy, and praise, that in going to eat meat; to buy, or sell; to meet a friend; or thwart an adversary; to communicate a piece of news or buy a book, he celebrates the arrival of an inconceivably remote purpose and law at last on the shores of Being, and into the ripeness and term of Nature. And because nothing chances, but all is locked and wheeled and chained in Law, in these motes and dust he can read the writing of the True Life and of a startling sublimity.

—JOURNAL, 1838

Have you ever found "a rock of diamonds" in "a day of facts"? Do you find that most days are prosaic and dull?

MARCH 20

Few men know how to take a walk. The qualifications of a professor are endurance, plain clothes, old shoes, an eye for nature, good humor, vast curiosity, good speech, good silence, and nothing too much.... It is a fine art, requiring rare gifts and much experience. No man is suddenly a good walker. Many men begin with good resolution, but they do not hold out. These we call apprentices. And I have sometimes thought it would be well to publish an Art of Walking, with easy lessons for beginners. Those who persist from year to year, and obtain at last an intimacy with the country, and know all the good points within ten miles, with the seasons for visiting each, know the lakes, the hills, where grapes, berries and nuts,— where the rare plants are; where the best botanic ground and where the noblest landscapes are seen, and are learning all the time;—these we call professors.

—COUNTRY LIFE

Do you know how to take a walk? Are you a beginner, a professor, or somewhere in between?

MARCH 21

We divorce ourselves from nature; we hide ourselves in cities and lose the affecting spectacle of Day and Night which she cheers and instructs her children withal. We pave the earth for miles with stones and forbid the grass. We build street on street all round the horizon and shut out the sky and the wind; false and costly tastes are generated for wise and cheap ones; thousands are poor and cannot see the face of the world; the senses are impaired, and the susceptibility to beauty; and life made vulgar. Our feeling in the presence of nature is an admonishing hint. Go and hear in a woodland valley the harmless roarings of the South wind and see the shining boughs of the trees in the sun, the swift sailing clouds, and you shall think a man is a fool to be mean and unhappy when every day is made illustrious by these splendid shows. Then falls the enchanting night: all the trees are wind-harps: out shine the stars: and we say, Blessed be light and darkness, ebb and flow, cold and heat, these restless pulsations of nature which throb for us. In the presence of nature a man of feeling is not suffered to lose sight of the instant creation. The world was not made a great while ago. Nature is an Eternal Now.

—HUMAN CULTURE

Do you think that "we divorce ourselves from nature"? How can we restore the relationship?

Each man has his own vocation. The talent is the call. There is one direction in which all space is open to him. He has faculties silently inviting him thither to endless exertion. He is like a ship in a river; he runs against obstructions on every side but one; on that side all obstruction is taken away, and he sweeps serenely over a deepening channel into an infinite sea. This talent and this call depend on his organization, or the mode in which the general soul incarnates itself in him. He inclines to do something which is easy to him, and good when it is done, but which no other man can do. He has no rival. For the more truly he consults his own powers, the more difference will his work exhibit from the work of any other. His ambition is exactly proportioned to his powers. The height of the pinnacle is determined by the breadth of the base. Every man has this call of the power to do somewhat unique, and no man has any other call. The pretense that he has another call, a summons by name and personal election and outward "signs that mark him extraordinary, and not in the roll of common men," is fanaticism, and betrays obtuseness to perceive that there is one mind in all the individuals, and no respect of persons therein.

—SPIRITUAL LAWS

Do you have your own destined vocation? Have you found it yet?

Life itself is a mixture of power and form, and will not bear the least excess of either. To finish the moment, to find the journey's end in every step of the road, to live the greatest number of good hours, is wisdom. It is not the part of men, but of fanatics, or of mathematicians, if you will, to say, that, the shortness of life considered, it is not worth caring whether for so short a duration we were sprawling in want, or sitting high. Since our office is with moments, let us husband them. Five minutes of today are worth as much to me, as five minutes in the next millennium. Let us be poised, and wise, and our own, today. Let us treat the men and women well: treat them as if they were real: perhaps they are. Men live in their fancy, like drunkards whose hands are too soft and tremulous for successful labor. It is a tempest of fancies, and the only ballast I know, is a respect to the present hour. Without any shadow of doubt, amidst this vertigo of shows and politics, I settle myself ever the firmer in the creed, that we should not postpone and refer and wish, but do broad justice where we are, by whomsoever we deal with, accepting our actual companions and circumstances, however humble or odious, as the mystic officials to whom the universe has delegated its whole pleasure for us.

— EXPERIENCE

How do you husband your moments? What does it mean to "do broad justice where we are"?

We live in a transition period, when the old faiths which comforted nations, and not only so, but made nations, seem to have spent their force.... The fatal trait is the divorce between religion and morality. Here are know-nothing religions, or churches that proscribe intellect; scortatory religions; slaveholding and slave-trading religions; and, even in the decent populations, idolatries wherein the whiteness of the ritual covers scarlet indulgence. The lover of the old religion complains that our contemporaries, scholars as well as merchants, succumb to a great despair,—have corrupted into a timorous conservatism, and believe in nothing. In our large cities, the population is godless, materialized,—no bond, no fellow-feeling, no enthusiasm. These are not men, but hungers, thirsts, fevers, and appetites walking. How is it people manage to live on,—so aimless as they are?... There is no faith in the intellectual, none in the moral universe. There is faith in chemistry, in meat, and wine, in wealth, in machinery, in the steam-engine, galvanic battery, turbine-wheels, sewing machines, and in public opinion, but not in divine causes. A silent revolution has loosed the tension of the old religious sects, and, in place of the gravity and permanence of those societies of opinion, they run into freak and extravagance.... From this change, and in the momentary absence of any religious genius that could offset the immense material activity, there is a feeling that religion is gone.

— WORSHIP

Are we living in a time when traditional religions have spent their force? Has skepticism replaced faith?

The world is always opulent; the oracles are never silent; but it requires that the receiver should by a happy temperance be brought into that top of condition, that frolic health, that he can easily take and give out again these fine communications. The trees in my garden are exposed to innumerable enemies, to blight, cold, insects, wounds; and many arts of cure are practiced; but the one royal cure is the thrifty tree, which outgrows blight, insects, and wounds. Every thing sound, lasting, and fit for men, the divine Power has marked with this stamp. What delights, what Emancipates, not what scares and pains us, is wise and good, in speech, writing and the arts. For, truly, the Heart at the center of the Universe, with every throb, hurls the flood of happiness into every artery, and vein, and veinlet, so that the whole system is inundated with the tides of joy. The plenty of the poorest place is too great; the harvest cannot be gathered. Every sound ends in music: The edge of every surface is tinged with prismatic rays.

—THE POWERS AND LAWS OF THOUGHT

Have you experienced the opulence of the world? Do you feel "the Heart at the center of the Universe" throbbing in you?

The weight of the universe is pressed down on the shoulders of each moral agent to hold him to his task. The only path of escape known in all the worlds of God is performance. You must do your work, before you shall be released.... And so I think that the last lesson of life, the choral song which rises from all elements and all angels, is, a voluntary obedience, a necessitated freedom. Man is made of the same atoms as the world is, he shares the same impressions, predispositions, and destiny. When his mind is illuminated, when his heart is kind, he throws himself joyfully into the sublime order, and does, with knowledge, what the stones do by structure.

— WORSHIP

Is "the last lesson of life" "a voluntary obedience, a necessitated freedom"? Can you throw yourself "joyfully into the sublime order"?

MARCH 27

Here among the mountains the pinions of thought should be strong and one should see the errors of men from a calmer height of love and wisdom. What is the message that is given me to communicate next Sunday? Religion in the mind is not credulity and in the practice is not form. It is a life. It is the order and soundness of a man. It is not something else *to be got*, to be *added*, but is a new life of those faculties you have. It is to do right. It is to love, it is to serve, it is to think, it is to be humble.

—JOURNAL, 1832

Do you agree with Emerson that religion is neither doctrine nor ritual, but rather "a new life of those faculties you have"? Have you experienced religion in this way?

The Indian teaching through its cloud of legends has yet a simple and grand religion like a queenly countenance seen through a rich veil. It teaches to speak the truth, love others as yourself, and to despise trifles. The East is grand and makes Europe appear the land of trifles. Identity Identity! friend and foe are of one stuff, and the stuff is such and so much that the variations of surface are unimportant. All is for the soul, and the soul is Vishnu; and animals and stars are transient paintings; and light is whitewash; and durations are deceptive; and form is imprisonment and heaven itself a decoy. That which the soul seeks is resolution into Being above form, out of Tartarus and out of Heaven; liberation from existence is its name. Cheerful and noble is the genius of this cosmogony. Hari is always gentle and serene,—he translates to heaven the hunter who has accidentally shot him in his human form; he pursues his sports with boors and milkmaids at the cow-pens; all his games are benevolent, and he enters into flesh to relieve the burdens of the world.

—JOURNAL, 1846

Have you found wisdom or inspiration in Eastern literature?
Do you believe, as the Hindus do, in the identity of all things?

Neither miracle nor magic nor any religious tradition, not the immortality of the private soul is incredible, after we have experienced an insight, a thought. I think it comes to some men but once in their life, sometimes a religious impulse, sometimes an intellectual insight. But what we want is consecutiveness. 'T is with us a flash of light, then a long darkness, then a flash again. The separation of our days by sleep almost destroys identity. Could we but turn these fugitive sparkles into an astronomy of Copernican worlds! With most men, scarce a link of memory holds yesterday and today together. Their house and trade and family serve them as ropes to give a course of continuity. But they have forgotten the thoughts of yesterday; they say today what occurs to them, and something else tomorrow. This insecurity of possession, this quick ebb of power,—as if life were a thunder-storm wherein you can see by a flash the horizon, and then cannot see your hand,—tantalizes us. We cannot make the inspiration consecutive. A glimpse, a point of view that by its brightness excludes the purview is granted, but no panorama. A fuller inspiration should cause the point to flow and become a line, should bend the line and complete the circle.

—INSPIRATION

Do you find it difficult to hold on to inspiration and insight? Do you wish for consecutiveness of vision in your life?

Life is a search after power; and this is an element with which the world is so saturated,—there is no chink or crevice in which it is not lodged,—that no honest seeking goes unrewarded. A man should prize events and possessions as the ore in which this fine material is found; and he can well afford to let events and possessions, and the breath of the body go, if their value has been added to him in the shape of power. If he have secured the elixir, he can spare the wide gardens from which it was distilled. A cultivated man, wise to know and bold to perform, is the end to which nature works, and the education of the will is the flowering and result of all this geology and astronomy.

—POWER

Do you agree that "life is a search after power"? What does power mean to you?

MARCH 31

All goes to show that the soul in man is not an organ, but animates and exercises all the organs; is not a function, like the power of memory, of calculation, of comparison, but uses these as hands and feet; is not a faculty, but a light; is not the intellect or the will, but the master of the intellect and the will; is the background of our being, in which they lie,—an immensity not possessed and that cannot be possessed. From within or from behind, a light shines through us upon things, and makes us aware that we are nothing, but the light is all. A man is the fasade of a temple wherein all wisdom and all good abide. What we commonly call man, the eating, drinking, planting, counting man, does not, as we know him, represent himself, but misrepresents himself. Him we do not respect, but the soul, whose organ he is, would he let it appear through his action, would make our knees bend. When it breathes through his intellect, it is genius; when it breathes through his will, it is virtue; when it flows through his affection, it is love. And the blindness of the intellect begins, when it would be something of itself. The weakness of the will begins when the individual would be something of himself. All reform aims, in some one particular, to let the soul have its way through us; in other words, to engage us to obey.

— THE OVER-SOUL

How would you describe the soul? How do you get in touch with it?

APRIL

Meditations

APRIL 1

It is a secret which every intellectual man quickly learns, that, beyond the energy of his possessed and conscious intellect, he is capable of a new energy (as of an intellect doubled on itself), by abandonment to the nature of things; that, beside his privacy of power as an individual man, there is a great public power, on which he can draw, by unlocking, at all risks, his human doors, and suffering the ethereal tides to roll and circulate through him: then is he caught up into the life of the Universe, his speech is thunder, his thought is law, and his words are universally intelligible as the plants and animals. The poet knows that he speaks adequately, then, only when he speaks somewhat wildly, or, "with the flower of the mind;" not with the intellect, used as an organ, but with the intellect released from all service, and suffered to take its direction from its celestial life; or, as the ancients were wont to express themselves, not with the intellect alone, but with the intellect inebriated by nectar. As the traveler who has lost his way, throws his reins on his horse's neck, and trusts to the instinct of the animal to find his road, so must we do with the divine animal who carries us through this world. For if in any manner we can stimulate this instinct, new passages are opened for us into nature, the mind flows into and through things hardest and highest, and the metamorphosis is possible.

— THE POET

Is there "great public power" that you can draw upon? Have you ever wanted to trust yourself to "the nature of things"?

APRIL 2

We must walk as guests in nature,—not impassioned, but cool and disengaged. A man should try time, and his face should wear the expression of a just judge, who has nowise made up his opinion, who fears nothing and even hopes nothing, but who puts nature and fortune on their merits: he will hear the case out, and then decide. For all melancholy, as all passion, belongs to the exterior life. Whilst a man is not grounded in the divine life by his proper roots, he clings by some tendrils of affection to society,—mayhap to what is best and greatest in it, and in calm times it will not appear that he is adrift and not moored; but let any shock take place in society, any revolution of custom, of law, of opinion, and at once his type of permanence is shaken. The disorder of his neighbors appears to him universal disorder; chaos is come again. But in truth he was already a driving wreck, before the wind arose which only revealed to him his vagabond state. If a man is centered, men and events appear to him a fair image or reflection of that which he knoweth beforehand in himself. If any perversity or profligacy break out in society, he will join with others to avert the mischief, but it will not arouse resentment or fear, because he discerns its impassable limits.

—THE TRAGIC

Have you ever considered detachment a virtue? What grounds you when all is shaken and lost?

Nature seems further to reply, 'I have ventured so great a stake as my success, in no single creature. I have not yet arrived at any end. The gardener aims to produce a fine peach or pear, but my aim is the health of the whole tree,—root, stem, leaf, flower, and seed,—and by no means the pampering of a monstrous pericarp at the expense of all the other functions.' In short, the spirit and peculiarity of that impression nature makes on us, is this, that it does not exist to any one or to any number of particular ends, but to numberless and endless benefit; that there is in it no private will, no rebel leaf or limb, but the whole is expressed by one superincumbent tendency, obeys that redundancy or excess of life which in conscious beings we call *ecstasy*.

—THE METHOD OF NATURE

Do you see yourself as a product of the redundancy or excess of life? Is there anything ecstatic in your life?

APRIL 4

The sinew and heart of man seem to be drawn out, and we are become timorous, desponding whimperers. We are afraid of truth, afraid of fortune, afraid of death, and afraid of each other. Our age yields no great and perfect persons. We want men and women who shall renovate life and our social state, but we see that most natures are insolvent, cannot satisfy their own wants, have an ambition out of all proportion to their practical force, and do lean and beg day and night continually. Our housekeeping is mendicant, our arts, our occupations, our marriages, our religion, we have not chosen, but society has chosen for us. We are parlor soldiers. We shun the rugged battle of fate, where strength is born.

—Self-Reliance

Do you see any today who shall "renovate life and our social state"? Are you a "parlor soldier"?

APRIL 5

There are no fixtures in nature. The universe is fluid and volatile. Permanence is but a word of degrees. Our globe seen by God is a transparent law, not a mass of facts. The law dissolves the fact and holds it fluid. Our culture is the predominance of an idea which draws after it this train of cities and institutions. Let us rise into another idea: they will disappear.... New arts destroy the old. See the investment of capital in aqueducts made useless by hydraulics; fortifications, by gunpowder; roads and canals, by railways; sails, by steam; steam by electricity. You admire this tower of granite, weathering the hurts of so many ages. Yet a little waving hand built this huge wall, and that which builds is better than that which is built. The hand that built can topple it down much faster. Better than the hand, and nimbler, was the invisible thought which wrought through it; and thus ever, behind the coarse effect, is a fine cause, which, being narrowly seen, is itself the effect of a finer cause. Everything looks permanent until its secret is known.

—Circles

Which, in Emerson's view, are more powerful, thoughts or things? Do you agree? Can you name examples?

APRIL 6

Although knaves win in every political struggle, although society seems to be delivered over from the hands of one set of criminals into the hands of another set of criminals, as fast as the government is changed, and the march of civilization is a train of felonies,—yet, general ends are somehow answered.... Through the years and the centuries, through evil agents, through toys and atoms, a great and beneficent tendency irresistibly streams. Let a man learn to look for the permanent in the mutable and fleeting; let him learn to bear the disappearance of things he was wont to reverence without losing his reverence; let him learn that he is here, not to work but to be worked upon; and that, though abyss open under abyss, and opinion displace opinion, all are at last contained in the Eternal Cause: "If my bark sink, 'tis to another sea."

—MONTAIGNE; OR, THE SKEPTIC

Do you believe that "a great and beneficent tendency irresistibly streams"? Can you see the permanent in the changeable and fleeting?

APRIL 7

In matters of religion, men eagerly fasten their eyes on the differences between their creed and yours, whilst the charm of the study is in finding the agreements and identities in all the religions of men. What is essential to the theologian is, that whilst he is select in his opinions, severe in his search for truth, he shall be broad in his sympathies,—not allow himself to be excluded from any church.... Be not betrayed into undervaluing the churches which annoy you by their bigoted claims. They too were real churches. They answered to their times the same need as your rejection of them does to ours.... I agree with them more than I disagree. I agree with their heart and motive; my discontent is with their limitations and surface and language.... Anything but unbelief, anything but losing hold of the moral intuitions, as betrayed in the clinging to a form of devotion or a theological dogma; as if it was the liturgy, or the chapel, that was sacred, and not justice and humility and the loving heart and serving hand.

— THE PREACHER

Do you agree with Emerson that the essence of religion is ethics? Do you focus on the differences or similarities between religious traditions?

APRIL 8

The days are made on a loom whereof the warp and woof are past and future time. They are majestically dressed, as if every god brought a thread to the skyey web. 'Tis pitiful the things by which we are rich or poor,—a matter of coins, coats and carpets, a little more or less stone, or wood, or paint, the fashion of a cloak or hat.... But the treasures which Nature spent itself to amass,—...these, not like a glass bead, or the coins or carpets, are given immeasurably to all.

—WORKS AND DAYS

What treasures "are given immeasurably to all"? What things make you rich or poor?

A believer in Unity, a seer of Unity, I yet behold two. Whilst I feel myself in sympathy with Nature and rejoice with greatly beating heart in the course of Justice and Benevolence over-powering me, I yet find little access to this Me of Me. I fear what shall befall: I am not enough a party to the great order to be tranquil. I hope and I fear; I do not see. At one time I am a Doer. A divine life I create, scenes and persons around and for me, and unfold my thought by a perpetual, successive projection. At least I so say, I so feel. But presently I return to the habitual attitude of suffering. I behold; I bask in beauty; I await; I wonder; where is my godhead now? This is the Male and Female principle in nature. One Man, male and female, created he him. Hard it is to describe God, it is harder to describe the Individual.

—JOURNAL, 1837

Do you believe in unity? Do you find it difficult, as Emerson apparently does, to hold on to that thought? Why is it so difficult to do so?

APRIL 10

I write anecdotes of the intellect; a sort of Farmer's Almanac of mental moods. I confine my ambition to true reporting of its play in natural action, though I should get only one new fact in a year. I cannot myself use that systematic form which is reckoned essential in treating the science of the mind. But if one can say so without arrogance, I might suggest that he who contents himself with dotting a fragmentary curve, recording only what facts he has observed, without attempting to arrange them within one outline, follows a system also,—a system as grand as any other, though he does not interfere with its vast curves by prematurely forcing them into a circle or ellipse, but only draws that arc which he clearly sees, or perhaps at a later observation a remote curve of the same orbit, and waits for a new opportunity, well assured that these observed arcs will consist with each other.

—Natural History of the Intellect

What kind of thinker are you? How would you describe your system of thought?

APRIL 11

The stationariness of religion; the assumption that the age of inspiration is past, that the Bible is closed; the fear of degrading the character of Jesus by representing him as a man; indicate with sufficient clearness the falsehood of our theology. It is the office of a true teacher to show us that God is, not was; that He speaketh, not spake. The true Christianity,—a faith like Christ's in the infinitude of man,—is lost. None believeth in the soul of man, but only in some man or person old and departed. Ah me! no man goeth alone. All men go in flocks to this saint or that poet, avoiding the God who seeth in secret. They cannot see in secret; they love to be blind in public. They think society wiser than their soul, and know not that one soul, and their soul, is wiser than the whole world.... Once leave your own knowledge of God, your own sentiment, and take secondary knowledge, as St. Paul's, or George Fox's, or Swedenborg's, and you get wide from God with every year this secondary form lasts, and if, as now, for centuries,—the chasm yawns to that breadth, that men can scarcely be convinced there is in them anything divine.

—THE DIVINITY SCHOOL ADDRESS

Do you believe that "the age of inspiration is past"? Do you think, as Emerson does, that religion is too derivative?

APRIL 12

We feel defrauded of the retribution due to evil acts, because the criminal adheres to his vice and contumacy, and does not come to a crisis or judgment anywhere in visible nature.... Has he therefore outwitted the law? Inasmuch as he carries the malignity and the lie with him, he so far deceases from nature. In some manner there will be a demonstration of the wrong to the understanding also; but should we not see it, this deadly deduction makes square the eternal account. Neither can it be said, on the other hand, that the gain of rectitude must be bought by any loss. There is no penalty to virtue; no penalty to wisdom; they are proper additions of being. In a virtuous action, I properly *am*; in a virtuous act, I add to the world; I plant into deserts conquered from Chaos and Nothing, and see the darkness receding on the limits of the horizon. There can be no excess to love; none to knowledge; none to beauty, when these attributes are considered in the purest sense. The soul refuses limits, and always affirms an Optimism, never a Pessimism.

—Compensation

Does the criminal who goes uncaught outwit the law? Is there a price to be paid for vice and evil?

APRIL 13

What is the hardest task in the world? To think. I would put myself in the attitude to look in the eye an abstract truth, and I cannot. I blench and withdraw on this side and on that. I seem to know what he meant who said, No man can see God face to face and live.... We say, I will walk abroad, and the truth will take form and clearness to me. We go forth, but cannot find it. It seems as if we needed only the stillness and composed attitude of the library to seize the thought. But we come in, and are as far from it as at first. Then, in a moment, and unannounced, the truth appears. A certain, wandering light appears, and is the distinction, the principle, we wanted. But the oracle comes, because we had previously laid siege to the shrine. It seems as if the law of the intellect resembled that law of nature by which we now inspire, now expire the breath; by which the heart now draws in, then hurls out the blood,—the law of undulation. So now you must labor with your brains, and now you must forbear your activity and see what the great Soul showeth.

— INTELLECT

Do you find it hard to think? How do you lay "siege to the shrine" of intellect?

APRIL 14

Let us build altars to the Beautiful Necessity, which secures that all is made of one piece; that plaintiff and defendant, friend and enemy, animal and planet, food and eater, are of one kind.... Why should we fear to be crushed by savage elements, we who are made up of the same elements? Let us build to the Beautiful Necessity, which makes man brave in believing that he cannot shun a danger that is appointed, nor incur one that is not; to the Necessity which rudely or softly educates him to the perception that there are no contingencies; that Law rules throughout existence, a Law which is not intelligent but intelligence,—not personal nor impersonal,—it disdains words and passes understanding; it dissolves persons; it vivifies nature; yet solicits the pure in heart to draw on all its omnipotence.

—FATE

Can you affirm a "Beautiful Necessity" in the workings of nature and human affairs? Do you agree with Emerson that "Law rules throughout existence"?

Reform is a vital function. It is not an old impulse by which we move, like a stone thrown into the air, but by an incessant impulse like that of gravitation. We are not potted and buried in our bodies, but every body is newly created from day to day, and every moment. Just as much life, so much is the power it exerts. . . . What we call preservation of the body is re-creation. There is no death in nature, but only passing of life from this to that: decomposition is recomposition; and cholera and palsy are the conversion of old organization into buds and embryos of new. To the poet, the world is virgin soil, all new. All is practicable. The men are ready for virtue. It is always time to do right. He is a recommencer and affirms. Reformers are our benefactors, our practical poets, hindering us of absurdity, and self-stultification.

—Reform

Do you agree that "reform is a vital function"? Can you point to examples of reformers? Are you a reformer?

One more trait of true success. The good mind chooses what is positive, what is advancing,—embraces the affirmative. Our system is one of poverty. 'Tis presumed...there is but one Shakespeare, one Homer, one Jesus,—not that all are or shall be inspired. But we must begin by affirming. Truth and goodness subsist forevermore. It is true there is evil and good, night and day: but these are not equal. The day is great and final. The night is for the day, but the day is not for the night.

—Success

Do you believe, as Emerson does, that the positive in life outweighs the negative? Do you consider yourself an affirmative, positive sort of person?

APRIL 17

This delight we all take in every show of night or day, of field or forest or sea or city, down to the lowest particulars is not without sequel though we be as yet only wishers and gazers not at all knowing what we want. We are predominated herein as elsewhere by an upper wisdom and resemble those great discoverers who are haunted for years, sometimes from infancy with a passion for the fact or class of facts in which the secret lies which they are destined to unlock and they let it not go until the blessing is won. So these sunsets and starlights, these swamps and rocks, these bird notes and animal forms off which we cannot get our eyes and ears but hover still as moths round a lamp are no doubt a Sanskrit cipher covering the whole religious history of the Universe, and presently we shall read it off into action and character. The pastures are full of ghosts for me, the morning woods full of angels. Now and then they give me a broad hint. Every natural fact is trivial until it becomes symbolical or moral.

—JOURNAL, 1840

What do the elements of nature symbolize for you? What ghosts and angels do you find in the pastures and woods?

We teach boys to be such men as we are. We do not teach them to aspire to be all they can. We do not give them a training as if we believed in their noble nature. We scarce educate their bodies. We do not train the eye and the hand. We exercise their understandings to the apprehension and comparison of some facts, to a skill in numbers, in words; we aim to make accountants, attorneys, engineers; but not to make able, earnest, great-hearted men. The great object of Education should be commensurate with the object of life. It should be a moral one; to teach self-trust; to inspire the youthful man with an interest in himself: with a curiosity touching his own nature; to acquaint him with the resources of his mind, and to teach him that there is all his strength, and to inflame him with a piety towards the Grand Mind in which he lives. Thus would education conspire with the Divine Providence. A man is a little thing whilst he works by and for himself, but, when he gives voice to the rules of love and justice, is godlike, his word is current in all countries; and all men, though his enemies, are made his friends and obey it as their own.

—Education

What is the object of education? Where does one get such an education as Emerson describes?

APRIL 19

"Miracles have ceased." Have they indeed? When? They had not ceased this afternoon when I walked into the wood and got into bright, miraculous sunshine in shelter from the roaring wind. Who sees a pine-cone, or the turpentine exuding from the tree, or a leaf, the unit of vegetation, fall from its bough as if it said, "The year is finished," or hears in the quiet piney glen the Chickadee chirping his cheerful note, or walks along the leafy promontory-like ridges which like natural causeways traverse the morass, or gazes upward at the rushing clouds, or downward at a moss or a stone and says to himself, "Miracles have ceased"?

—JOURNAL, 1838

When was the last time you noticed a miracle? What was it?

APRIL 20

By doing his work, he makes the need felt which he can supply, and creates the taste by which he is enjoyed. By doing his own work, he unfolds himself. It is the vice of our public speaking that it has not abandonment. Somewhere, not only every orator but every man should let out all the length of all the reins; should find or make a frank and hearty expression of what force and meaning is in him. The common experience is, that the man fits himself as well as he can to the customary details of that work or trade he falls into, and tends it as a dog turns a spit. Then is he a part of the machine he moves; the man is lost. Until he can manage to communicate himself to others in his full stature and proportion, he does not yet find his vocation. He must find in that an outlet for his character, so that he may justify his work to their eyes. If the labor is mean, let him by his thinking and character make it liberal. Whatever he knows and thinks, whatever in his apprehension is worth doing, that let him communicate, or men will never know and honor him aright.

—Spiritual Laws

In there some place in your life where you can "let out all the reins"? Must you fit yourself into the customary details of your work or trade?

APRIL 21

The fine young people despise life, but in me, and in such as with me are free from dyspepsia, and to whom a day is a sound and solid good, it is a great excess of politeness to look scornful and to cry for company. I am grown by sympathy a little eager and sentimental, but leave me alone, and I should relish every hour and what it brought me, the pot-luck of the day, as heartily as the oldest gossip in the bar-room. I am thankful for small mercies. I compared notes with one of my friends who expects everything of the universe, and is disappointed when anything is less than the best, and I found that I begin at the other extreme, expecting nothing, and am always full of thanks for moderate goods. I accept the clangor and jangle of contrary tendencies. I find my account in sots and bores also. They give a reality to the circumjacent picture, which such a vanishing meteorous appearance can ill spare. In the morning I awake, and find the old world, wife, babes, and mother, Concord and Boston, the dear old spiritual world, and even the dear old devil not far off. If we will take the good we find, asking no questions, we shall have heaping measures. The great gifts are not got by analysis. Everything good is on the highway. The middle region of our being is the temperate zone. We may climb into the thin and cold realm of pure geometry and lifeless science, or sink into that of sensation. Between these extremes is the equator of life, of thought, of spirit, of poetry,—a narrow belt.

— Experience

Are you able to relish the pot-luck of the day? Do you agree with Emerson that life is best lived in "the temperate zone"?

APRIL 22

You say, there is no religion now. 'Tis like saying in rainy weather, there is no sun, when at that moment we are witnessing one of his superlative effects. The religion of the cultivated class now, to be sure, consists in an avoidance of acts and engagements which it was once their religion to assume. But this avoidance will yield spontaneous forms in their due hour. There is a principle which is the basis of things, which all speech aims to say, and all action to evolve, a simple, quiet, undescribed, undescribable presence, dwelling very peacefully in us, our rightful lord: we are not to do, but to let do; not to work, but to be worked upon; and to this homage there is a consent of all thoughtful and just men in all ages and conditions. To this sentiment belong vast and sudden enlargements of power. 'Tis remarkable that our faith in ecstasy consists with total inexperience of it. It is the order of the world to educate with accuracy the senses and the understanding; and the enginery at work to draw out these powers in priority, no doubt, has its office. But we are never without a hint that these powers are mediate and servile, and that we are one day to deal with real being,—essences with essences.

— WORSHIP

Do you find it difficult to let go, "not to do, but to let do"? Is your faith still growing?

Under every leaf, is the bud of a new leaf; and, not less, under every thought, is a newer thought. Every reform is only a mask, under cover of which a more terrible reform, which dares not yet name itself, advances. The plant absorbs much nourishment from the ground, in order to repair its own waste by exhalation, and keep itself good. Increase its food, and it becomes fertile. The mind is first only receptive. Surcharge it with thoughts, in which it delights, and it becomes active. The moment a man begins not to be convinced, that moment he begins to convince. In the orchard, many trees send out a moderate shoot in the first summer heat, and stop. They look, all summer, as if they would presently burst the bud again, and grow; but they do not. The fine tree continues to grow. The same thing happens in the man. The commonest remark, if the man could only extend it a little, would make him a genius; but the thought is prematurely checked and grows no more.

—THE RELATION OF INTELLECT TO NATURAL SCIENCE

Is there renewal and reform in you? Do you find your thoughts prematurely checked?

How hard to command the soul or to solicit the soul. Many of our actions, many of mine are done to solicit the soul. Put away your flesh, put on your faculties. I would think—I would feel. I would be the vehicle of that divine principle that lurks within and of which life has afforded only glimpses enough to assure me of its being. We know little of its laws—but we have observed that a north wind clear cold with its scattered fleet of drifting clouds braced the body and seemed to reflect a similar abyss of spiritual heaven between clouds in our minds; or a brisk conversation moved this mighty deep or a word in a book was made an omen of by the mind and surcharged with meaning or an oration or a south wind or a college or a cloudy lonely walk.... And having this experience we strive to avail ourselves of it and propitiate the divine inmate to speak to us again out of clouds and darkness. Truly whilst it speaketh not man is a pitiful being. He whistles, eats, sleeps, gets his gun, makes his bargain, lounges, sins, and when all is done is yet wretched. Let the soul speak, and all this driveling and these toys are thrown aside and man listens like a child.

—JOURNAL, 1832

Have you tried "to command" your soul to speak to you? Have you been successful? Are you unfulfilled by the activities that constitute the bulk of your days?

Do not be too timid and squeamish about your actions. All life is an experiment. The more experiments you make the better. What if they are a little course, and you may get your coat soiled or torn? What if you do fail, and get fairly rolled in the dirt once or twice? Up again, you shall nevermore be so afraid of a tumble. This matter of the lectures, for instance. The engagement drives your thoughts and studies to a head, and enables you to do somewhat not otherwise practicable; that is the action. Then there is the reaction; for when you bring your discourse to your auditory, it shows differently. You have more power than you thought of, or less. The thing fits or does not fit; is good or detestable.

—JOURNAL, 1842

What is your attitude toward failure and personal disappointment? How do you react to the unpredictability of life?

APRIL 26

You are rightly fond of certain books or men that you have found to excite your reverence and emulation. But none of these can compare with the greatness of that counsel which is open to you in happy solitude. I mean that there is for you the following of an inward leader,—a slow discrimination that there is for each a Best Counsel which enjoins the fit word and the fit act for every moment. And the path of each, pursued, leads to greatness. How grateful to find in man or woman a new emphasis of their own. But if the first rule is to obey your native bias, to accept that work for which you were inwardly formed,—the second rule is concentration, which doubles its force. Thus, if you are a scholar, be that. The same laws hold for you as for the laborer. The shoemaker makes a good shoe because he makes nothing else. Let the student mind his own charge; sedulously wait every morning for the news concerning the structure of the world which the spirit will give him.

—GREATNESS

What is your native bias, the work for which you were inwardly formed? Are you able to concentrate? Do you await "the news concerning the structure of the world"? What does it tell you?

To believe your own thought, to believe that what is true for you in your private heart is true for all men,—that is genius. Speak your latent conviction, and it shall be the universal sense; for the inmost in due time becomes the outmost,—and our first thought is rendered back to us by the trumpets of the Last Judgment. Familiar as the voice of the mind is to each, the highest merit we ascribe to Moses, Plato, and Milton is, that they set at naught books and traditions, and spoke not what men but what they thought. A man should learn to detect and watch that gleam of light which flashes across his mind from within, more than the lustre of the firmament of bards and sages. Yet he dismisses without notice his thought, because it is his. In every work of genius we recognize our own rejected thoughts: they come back to us with a certain alienated majesty.

—SELF-RELIANCE

Have your rejected thoughts ever come back to you in the words of another? Do you dismiss your own thoughts in deference to others?

APRIL 28

Before the revelations of the soul, Time, Space, and Nature shrink away. In common speech, we refer all things to time, as we habitually refer the immensely sundered stars to one concave sphere. And so we say that the Judgment is distant or near, that the Millennium approaches, that a day of certain political, moral, social reforms is at hand, and the like, when we mean, that, in the nature of things, one of the facts we contemplate is external and fugitive, and the other is permanent and connate with the soul. The things we now esteem fixed shall, one by one, detach themselves, like ripe fruit, from our experience, and fall. The wind shall blow them none knows whither. The landscape, the figures, Boston, London, are facts as fugitive as any institution past, or any whiff of mist or smoke, and so is society, and so is the world. The soul looketh steadily forwards, creating a world before her, leaving worlds behind her. She has no dates, nor rites, nor persons, nor specialties, nor men. The soul knows only the soul; the web of events is the flowing robe in which she is clothed.

—THE OVER-SOUL

Have you experienced "Time, Space, and Nature shrink away" before your own soul's revelations? What does it mean that the soul is beyond space and time?

APRIL 29

The only gift is a portion of thyself. Thou must bleed for me. Therefore the poet brings his poem; the shepherd, his lamb; the farmer, corn; the miner, a gem; the sailor, coral and shells; the painter, his picture; the girl, a handkerchief of her own sewing. This is right and pleasing, for it restores society in so far to its primary basis, when a man's biography is conveyed in his gift, and every man's wealth is an index of his merit. But it is a cold, lifeless business when you go to the shops to buy me something, which does not represent your life and talent, but a goldsmith's.

—Gifts

When was the last time you made a gift for someone? What gift can you make by your own hands?

APRIL 30

We are all believers in natural religion; we all agree that the health and integrity of man is self-respect, self-subsistency, a regard to natural conscience. All education is to accustom him to trust himself, discriminate between his higher and lower thoughts, exert the timid faculties until they are robust, and thus train him to self-help, until he ceases to be an underling, a tool, and becomes a benefactor. It think wise men wish their religion to be all of this kind, teaching the agent to go alone, not to hang on the world as a pensioner, a permitted person, but an adult, self-searching soul, brave to assist or resist a world: only humble and docile before the source of the wisdom he has discovered within him.

—SPEECH AT THE SECOND ANNUAL MEETING OF
THE FREE RELIGIOUS ASSOCIATION

Do you believe in natural religion? Are you a "self-searching soul, brave to assist or resist a world"?

MAY

Meditations

MAY 1

There is a sublime and friendly Destiny by which the human race is guided,—the race never dying, the individual never spared,—to results affecting masses and ages. Men are narrow and selfish, but the Genius or Destiny is not narrow, but beneficent. It is not discovered in their calculated and voluntary activity, but in what befalls, with or without their design. Only what is inevitable interests us, and it turns out that love and good are inevitable, and in the course of things.... This Genius, or Destiny, is of the sternest administration, though rumors exist of its secret tenderness. It may be styled a cruel kindness, serving the whole even to the ruin of the member; a terrible communist, reserving all profits to the community, without dividend to individuals. Its law is, you shall have everything as a member, nothing to yourself.

—THE YOUNG AMERICAN

Do you think "love and good are inevitable, and in the course of things"? Do you feel that, in spite of our personal losses, the tendency of nature is toward the good of the whole?

MAY 2

Nothing is fair or good alone.
I thought the sparrow's note from heaven,
Singing at dawn on the alder bough;
I brought him home, in his nest, at even;
He sings the song, but it cheers not now,
For I did not bring home the river and sky;—
He sang to my ear,—they sang to my eye.
The delicate shells lay on the shore;
The bubbles of the latest wave
Fresh pearls to their enamel gave;
And the bellowing of the savage sea
Greeted their safe escape to me.
I wiped away the weeds and foam,
I fetched my sea-born treasures home;
But the poor, unsightly, noisome things
Had left their beauty on the shore
With the sun and the sand and the wild uproar.

—Each and All

Have you had a similar experience? Why do shells look different at home than at the beach?

MAY 3

A man's genius, the quality that differences him from every other, the susceptibility to one class of influences, the selection of what is fit for him, the rejection of what is unfit, determines for him the character of the universe. A man is a method, a progressive arrangement; a selecting principle, gathering his like to him, wherever he goes. He takes only his own out of the multiplicity that sweeps and circles round him. He is like one of those booms which are set out from the shore on rivers to catch drift-wood, or like the loadstone amongst splinters of steel. Those facts, words, persons, which dwell in his memory without his being able to say why, remain, because they have a relation to him not less real for being as yet unapprehended.... What attracts my attention shall have it, as I will go to the man who knocks at my door, whilst a thousand persons, as worthy, go by it, to whom I give no regard. It is enough that these particulars speak to me. A few anecdotes, a few traits of character, manners, face, a few incidents, have an emphasis in your memory out of all proportion to their apparent significance, if you measure them by the ordinary standards. They relate to your gift. Let them have their weight, and do not reject them, and cast about for illustration and facts more usual in literature. What your heart thinks great is great. The soul's emphasis is always right.

—SPIRITUAL LAWS

Are we susceptible to only the influences that are meant for us? Are you as confident as Emerson that "the soul's emphasis is always right"?

MAY 4

Life is a search after power; and this is an element with which the world is so saturated,—there is no chink or crevice in which it is not lodged,—that no honest seeking goes unrewarded. A man should prize events and possessions as the ore in which this fine mineral is found; and he can well afford to let events and possessions, and the breath of the body go, if their value has been added to him in the shape of power. If he have secured the elixir, he can spare the wide gardens from which it was distilled. A cultivated man, wise to know and bold to perform, is the end to which nature works, and the education of the will is the flowering and result of all this geology and astronomy.

—POWER

How do you define power? Is your life a search for it?

MAY 5

A certain wandering light comes to me which I instantly perceive to be the Cause of Causes. It transcends all proving. It is itself the ground of being; and I see that it is not one and I another, but this is the life of my life. That is one fact, then; that in certain moments I have known that I existed directly from God, and am, as it were, his organ. And in my ultimate consciousness Am He. Then, secondly, the contradictory fact is familiar, that I am a surprised spectator and learner of all my life. This is the habitual posture of the mind,—beholding. But whenever the day dawns, the great day of truth on the soul, it comes with awful invitation to me to accept it, to blend with its aurora. Cannot I conceive the Universe with out a contradiction?

—JOURNAL, 1837

Have you ever felt that you were "God's organ"? Have you ever felt yourself on the outside of life looking in, wanting to accept life and "blend with its aurora"?

I conceive a man as always spoken to from behind, and unable to turn his head and see the speaker. In all the millions who have heard the voice, none ever saw the face. As children in their play run behind each other, and seize one by the ears and make him walk before them, so is the spirit our unseen pilot. That well-known voice speaks in all languages, governs all men, and none ever caught a glimpse of its form. If the man will exactly obey it, it will adopt him, so that he shall not any longer separate it from himself in his thought; he shall seem to be it, he shall be it. If he listen with insatiable ears, richer and greater wisdom is taught him, the sound swells to a ravishing music, he is borne away as with a flood, he becomes careless of his food and of his house, he is the fool of ideas, and leads a heavenly life. But if his eye is set on the things to be done, and not on the truth that is still taught, and for the sake of which the things are to be done, then the voice grows faint, and at last is but a humming in his ears. His health and greatness consist in his being the channel through which heaven flows to earth, in short, in the fullness in which an ecstatical state takes place in him.

—THE METHOD OF NATURE

Do you feel that you are "spoken to from behind"? What, if anything, have you heard?

MAY 7

In youth we are mad for persons. Childhood and youth see all the world in them. But the larger experience of man discovers the identical nature appearing through them all. Persons themselves acquaint us with the impersonal. In all conversation between two persons, tacit reference is made, as to a third party, to a common nature. That third party or common nature is not social; it is impersonal; is God. And so in groups where debate is earnest, and especially on high questions, the company become aware that the thought rises to an equal level in all bosoms, that all have a spiritual property in what was said, as well as the sayer. They all become wiser than they were. It arches over them like a temple, this unity of thought, in which every heart beats with nobler sense of power and duty, and thinks and acts with unusual solemnity. All are conscious of attaining to a higher self-possession. It shines for all.

—THE OVER-SOUL

Do you find that there is "a higher self-possession" in all earnest conversation, a greater knowledge than any one person possesses? Is conversation in this sense a spiritual practice for you?

MAY 8

Even the fury of material activity has some results friendly to moral health. The energetic action of the times develops individualism, and the religious appear isolated. I esteem this a step in the right direction. Heaven deals with us on no representative system. Souls are not saved in bundles. The Spirit saith to the man, "How is it with thee? Thee personally? Is it well? Is it ill?" For a great nature, it is a happiness to escape a religious training,—religion of character is so apt to be invaded. Religion must always be a crab fruit: it cannot be grafted and keep its wild beauty. "I have seen," said a traveler who had known the extremes of society, "I have seen human nature in all its forms, it is everywhere the same, but the wilder it is, the more virtuous."

— WORSHIP

What does "souls are not saved in bundles" mean to you?
Do you believe that "religion must always be a crab fruit"?

MAY 9

In all my lectures, I have taught one doctrine, namely, the infinitude of the private man. This, the people accept readily enough, and even with loud commendation, as long as I call the lecture, Art; or Politics; or Literature; or the Household; but the moment I call it Religion,—they are shocked, though it be only the application of the same truth which they receive everywhere else, to a new class of facts.

—JOURNAL, 1840

Do you believe, as Emerson does, that human potential is infinite? Are you shocked that he would apply the doctrine to religion?

By trusting your own heart, you shall gain more confidence in other men. For all our penny-wisdom, for all our soul-destroying slavery to habit, it is not to be doubted, that all men have sublime thoughts; that all men value the few real hours of life; they love to be heard; they love to be caught up into the vision of principles. We mark with light in the memory the few interviews we have had, in the dreary years of routine and of sin, with souls that made our souls wiser; that spoke what we thought; that told us what we knew; that gave us leave to be what we inly were.

—THE DIVINITY SCHOOL ADDRESS

Can you think of teachers or ministers who made your soul wiser? Do you wish "to be caught up into the vision of principles"?

MAY 11

The life of man is a self-evolving circle, which, from a ring imperceptibly small, rushes on all sides outwards to new and larger circles, and that without end. The extent to which this generation of circles, wheel without wheel, will go, depends on the force or truth of the individual soul. For it is the inert effort of each thought, having formed itself into a circular wave of circumstance,—as, for instance, an empire, rules of an art, a local usage, a religious rite,—to heap itself on that ridge, and to solidify and hem in the life. But if the soul is quick and strong, it bursts over that boundary on all sides, and expands another orbit on the great deep, which also runs up into a high wave, with attempt again to stop and to bind. But the heart refuses to be imprisoned; in its first and narrowest pulses, it already tends outward with a vast force, and to immense and innumerable expansions. Every ultimate fact is only the first of a new series. Every general law only a particular fact of some more general law presently to disclose itself. There is no outside, no inclosing wall, no circumference to us.

—Circles

How is your life "a self-evolving circle"? Are there examples in your life of the process Emerson describes in this passage?

Exaggeration is in the course of things. Nature sends no creature, no man into the world, without adding a small excess of his proper quality. Given the planet, it is still necessary to add the impulse; so, to every creature nature added a little violence of direction in its proper path, a shove to put it on its way; in every instance, a slight generosity, a drop too much. Without electricity the air would rot, and without this violence of direction, which men and women have, without a spice of bigot and fanatic, no excitement, no efficiency. We aim above the mark, to hit the mark. Every act hath some falsehood of exaggeration in it. And when now and then comes along some sad, sharp-eyed man, who sees how paltry a game is played, and refuses to play, but blabs the secret;—how then? is the bird flown? O no, the wary Nature sends a new troop of fairer forms, of lordlier youths, with a little more excess of direction to hold them fast to their several aim; makes them a little wrong-headed in that direction in which they are rightest, and on goes the game again with new whirl, for a generation or two more.

—NATURE

What quality do you possess in excess? How do you feel about this excess?

MAY 13

Last night the moon rose behind four distinct pine-tree tops in the distant woods and the night at ten was so bright that I walked abroad....Come out of your warm, angular house, re-sounding with few voices, into the grand, chill, instantaneous night, with such a Presence as a full moon in the clouds, and you are struck with poetic wonder. In the instant you leave be-hind all human relations, wife, mother and child, and live only with the savages,—water, air, light, carbon, lime, and granite....I become a moist, cold element. "Nature grows over me." Frogs pipe; waters far off tinkle; dry leaves hiss; grass bends and rustles, and I have died out of the human world and come to feel a strange, cold, aqueous, terraqueous, aerial, ethereal sympathy and existence. I sow the sun and moon for seeds.

—JOURNAL, 1845

Have you ever felt, in the presence of nature, that you have died out of the human world? Have you felt the strange kinship with nature that Emerson describes?

We have a debt to every great heart, to every fine genius; to those who put life and fortune on the cast of an act of justice; to those who have added new sciences; to those who have refined life by elegant pursuits. 'Tis the fine souls who serve us, and not what is called fine society. . . . There are other measures of self-respect for a man, than the number of clean shirts he puts on every day. Society wishes to be amused. I do not wish to be amused. I wish that life should not be cheap, but sacred. I wish the days to be as centuries, loaded, fragrant. Now we reckon them as bank-days, by some debt which is to be paid us, or which we are to pay, or some pleasure we are to taste. Is all we have to do to draw the breath in, and blow it out again?

—CONSIDERATIONS BY THE WAY

What are your measures of self-respect? How can we make life "not cheap, but sacred"?

God offers to every mind its choice between truth and repose. Take which you please,—you can never have both. Between these, as a pendulum, man oscillates. He in whom the love of repose predominates will accept the first creed, the first philosophy, the first political party he meets,—most likely his father's. He gets rest, commodity, and reputation; but he shuts the door of truth. He in whom the love of truth predominates will keep himself aloof from all moorings, and afloat. He will abstain from dogmatism, and recognize all the opposite negations, between which, as walls, his being is swung. He submits to the inconvenience of suspense and imperfect opinion, but he is a candidate for truth, as the other is not, and respects the highest law of his being.

—INTELLECT

Does repose or truth predominate in your mind? How difficult is it to keep "aloof from all moorings" and "abstain from dogmatism"?

MAY 16

All civil mankind have agreed in leaving one day for contemplation against six for practice. I hope that day will keep its honor and use. A wise man advises we should see to it that we read and speak two or three reasonable words, every day, amid the crowd of affairs and the noise of trifles. I should say boldly that we should astonish every day by a beam out of eternity; retire a moment to the grand secret we carry in our bosom, of inspiration from heaven. But certainly on this seventh let us be the children of liberty, of reason, of hope; refresh the sentiment; think as spirits think, who belong to the universe, whilst our feet walk in the streets of a little town and our hands work in a small knot of affairs. We shall find one result, I am sure,— a certain originality and a certain haughty liberty proceeding out of our retirement and self-communion which streets can never give, infinitely removed from all vaporing and bravado, and which yet is more than a match for any physical resistance. It is true that which they say of our New England oestrum, which will never let us stand or sit, but drives us like mad through the world. The calmest and most protected life cannot save us. We want some intercalated days, to bethink us and to derive order to our life from the heart. That should be the use of the Sabbath,—to check this headlong racing and put us in possession of ourselves once more, for love or for shame.

— THE PREACHER

Do you retire for a moment each day "to the grand secret we carry in our bosom, of inspiration from heaven"? How do you make use of the Sabbath?

MAY 17

Such are the days,—the earth is the cup, the sky is the cover, of the immense bounty of Nature which is offered us for our daily aliment; but what a force of *illusion* begins life with us and attends us to the end! We are coaxed, flattered and duped from morn to eve, from birth to death; and where is the old eye that ever saw through the deception? The Hindoos represent Maia, the illusory energy of Vishnu, as one of his principal attributes. As if, in this gale of warring elements which life is, it was necessary to bind souls to human life as mariners in a tempest lash themselves to the mast and bulwarks of a ship, and Nature employed certain illusions as her ties and straps,—a rattle, a doll, an apple, for a child; skates, a river, a boat, a horse, a gun, for the growing boy; and I will not begin to name those of the youth and adult, for they are numberless. Seldom and slowly the mask falls and the pupil is permitted to see that all is one stuff, cooked and painted under many counterfeit appearances.... This element of illusion lends all its force to hide the values of present time.

— WORKS AND DAYS

What illusions have you struggled with? How have you dispelled them?

MAY 18

Time, the consoler, time, the rich carrier of all changes, dries the freshest tears by obtruding new figures, new costumes, new roads, on our eye, new voices on our ear. As the west wind lifts up again the heads of the wheat which were bent down and lodged in the storm, and combs out the matted and dishevelled grass as it lay in night-locks on the ground, so we let in time as a drying wind into the seed-field of thoughts which are dark and wet, and low-bent. Time restores to them temper and elasticity. How fast we forget the blow that threatened to cripple us. Nature will not sit still; the faculties will do somewhat; new hopes spring, new affections twine, and the broken is whole again. Time consoles, but Temperament resists the impression of pain. Nature proportions her defense to the assault. Our human being is wonderfully plastic; if it cannot win this satisfaction here, it makes itself amends by running out there and winning that. It is like a stream of water, which, if dammed up on one bank, over-runs the other, and flows equally at its own convenience over sand, or mud, or marble. Most suffering is only apparent. We fancy it is torture: the patient has his own compensations.

— THE TRAGIC

What is your temperament with respect to pain and suffering? Do you agree with Emerson that most suffering is only apparent?

There is a time in every man's education when he arrives at the conviction that envy is ignorance; that imitation is suicide; that he must take himself for better, for worse, as his portion; that though the wide universe is full of good, no kernel of nourishing corn can come to him but through his toil bestowed on that plot of ground which is given to him to till. The power which resides in him is new in nature, and none but he knows what that is which he can do, nor does he know until he has tried. . . . Trust thyself: every heart vibrates to that iron string. Accept the place the divine providence has found for you, the society of your contemporaries, the connection of events. Great men have always done so, and confided themselves childlike to the genius of their age, betraying their perception that the absolutely trustworthy was seated at their heart, working through their hands, predominating in all their being. And we are now men, and must accept in the highest mind the same transcendent destiny; and not minors and invalids in a protected corner, not cowards fleeing before a revolution, but guides, redeemers, and benefactors, obeying the Almighty effort, and advancing on Chaos and the Dark.

—Self-Reliance

What "plot of ground" has been given you to till? Is what is in your heart absolutely trustworthy?

With such volatile elements to work in, 'tis no wonder if our estimates are loose and floating. We must work and affirm, but we have no guess of the value of what we say or do.... We fancy we have fallen into bad company and squalid condition, low debts, shoe-bills, broken glass to pay for, pots to buy, butcher's meat, sugar, milk and coal. "Set me some great task, ye gods! and I will show my spirit." "Not so," says the good Heaven; "plod and plough, vamp your old coats and hats, weave a shoe-string; great affairs and the best wine by and by." Well, 'tis all phantasm; and if we weave a yard of tape in all humility, and as well as we can, long hereafter we shall see it was no cotton tape at all, but some galaxy which we braided, and that the threads were Time and Nature.

—ILLUSIONS

Is it difficult to know the value of your work from the limited perspective of everyday life? What galaxy are you braiding with the time and resources you have been given?

MAY 21

A religion of the simplest elements; the first duties that everywhere exist, commanded by the primal sentiments, need no magnificent annunciation by ancient prophecy or special messengers attended by angels from the skies, but are born in the Indian and the Hottentot, and only need to be obeyed, in order to speak with a clearer voice, and to deliver the whole code of moral and spiritual life. I like to invite and to be invited to realism, to the simple truth, which never yet hurt anybody; to the riches of the poor; to the height of lowliness; to the luxury of the elements of water and bread; and to the highest heavens through this universal path. These to be all, or, perhaps, even the best. My intercourse has led me to believe that in solitude and obscurity this revelation is often made. But the children of God cannot communicate by speech that which they have known. These are things which words will not carry.

—Natural Religion

Is religion simple or complicated for you? Is it the result of an ancient prophesy or a present revelation? Is it natural and universal, or particular to different groups of people?

The inner life sits at home, and does not learn to do things, nor value these feats at all. 'Tis a quiet, wise perception. It loves truth, because it is itself real; it loves right, it knows nothing else; but it makes no progress; was as wise in our first memory of it as now; is just the same now in maturity and hereafter in age, it was in youth. We have grown to manhood and womanhood; we have powers, connection, children, reputations, professions: this makes no account of them all. It lives in the great present; it makes the present great. This tranquil, well-founded, wide-seeing soul is no express-rider, no attorney, no magistrate: it lies in the sun and broods on the world. A person of this temper once said to a man of much activity, "I will pardon you that you do so much, and you me that I do nothing."

—Success

Do you sense a tranquil, "wide-seeing soul" in you? What does it tell you about the way you should live your life?

I confess to a little distrust of that completeness of system which metaphysicians are apt to affect. 'T is the gnat grasping the world. All these exhaustive theories appear indeed a false and vain attempt to introvert and analyze the Primal Thought. That is upstream, and what a stream! Can you swim up Niagara Falls? We have invincible repugnance to introversion, to study of the eyes instead of that which the eyes see; and the belief of men is that the attempt is unnatural and is punished by loss of faculty. I share the belief that the natural direction of the intellectual powers is from within outward, and that just in proportion to the activity of thoughts on the study of outward objects, as architecture, or farming, or natural history, ships, animals, chemistry,— in that proportion the faculties of the mind had a healthy growth; but a study in the opposite direction had a damaging effect on the mind. Metaphysics is dangerous as a single pursuit. We should feel more confidence in the same results from the mouth of a man of the world. The inward analysis must be corrected by rough experience. Metaphysics must be perpetually reinforced by life; must be the observations of working man on working men; must be biography,—the record of some law whose working was surprised by the observer in natural action.

—NATURAL HISTORY OF INTELLECT

Do you share Emerson's skepticism that metaphysics can adequately "analyze the Primal Thought"? What does it mean that your philosophy of life should "be corrected by rough experience"?

MAY 24

[At Mount Auburn Cemetery.] I forsook the tombs and found a sunny hollow where the east wind could not blow and lay down against the side of a tree to most happy beholdings. At least I opened my eyes and let what would pass through them into the soul. I saw no more my relation how near and petty to Cambridge or Boston, I heeded no more what minute or hour our Massachusetts clocks might indicate—I saw only the noble earth on which I was born, with the great Star which warms and enlightens it. I saw the clouds that hang their significant drapery over us.—It was Day, that was all Heaven said. The pines glittered with their innumerable green needles in the light and seemed to challenge me to read their riddle. The drab-oak leaves of the last year turned their little somersets and lay still again. And the wind bustled high overhead in the forest top. This gay and grand architecture from the vault to the moss and lichen on which I lay who shall explain to me the laws of its proportions and adornments?

—JOURNAL, 1834

Have you had a mystical experience such as the one
Emerson describes? Where and under what circumstances
did it happen?

The craft with which the world is made, runs also into the mind and character of men. No man is quite sane; each has a vein of folly in his composition, a slight determination of blood to the head, to make sure of holding him hard to some one point which nature had taken to heart. Great causes are never tried on their merits; but the cause is reduced to particulars to suit the size of the partisans, and the contention is ever hottest on minor matters. Not less remarkable is the overfaith of each man in the importance of what he has to do or say. The poet, the prophet, has a higher value for what he utters than any hearer, and therefore it gets spoken.... Each prophet comes presently to identify himself with his thought, and to esteem his hat and shoes sacred. However this may discredit such persons with the judicious, it helps them with the people, as it gives heat, pungency, and publicity to their words.

—NATURE

What is "the vein of folly" in you? Can you think of poets, prophets, and politicians who fit Emerson's description?

We live in a transition period, when the old faiths which have educated, and comforted, and legislated for nations, and not only so, but have made the nations, seem to have spent their force, and to be comparatively powerless on the public and the private mind of Europe and America. Society is now full of fancy faiths, of gentlemen and of nations in search of religions. It seems to me, as if men stood craving a more stringent creed than any of the pale and enervating systems to which they had recourse. The Turk who believes that his doom is written on the iron leaf on the moment when he entered the world, and that he cannot alter it, rushes on the enemy's sword with undivided will. The Buddhist who finds gods masked in all his friends and enemies, and reads the issue of the conflict beforehand in the rank of the actors, is calm. The old Greek was respectable, and we are not yet able to forget his dramas,—who found the genius of tragedy in the conflict between Destiny and the strong *should*, and not like the moderns, in the weak *would*. And the natural remedy against this miscellany of knowledge and aim, this desultory universality of ours, this immense ground-juniper falling abroad, and not gathered up into any columnar tree, is, to substitute realism, for sentimentalism; a recognition of the simple and terrible laws, which, seen or unseen . . . pervade and govern.

— The Tendencies and Duties of Men of Thought

Do you agree with Emerson's estimate of modern faith? Is your faith strenuous—realistic and not sentimental—in the way that Emerson suggests?

I have complained that the acknowledgment of God's presence halts far behind the fact. What is it intended to be but the tribute to one without whose movings no tribute can be paid for no tributary can be? One without whom no man or beast or nature subsists; One who is the life of things and from whose creative will our life and the life of all creatures flows every moment, wave after wave, like the successive beams that every moment issue from the Sun. Such is God, or he is nothing. What is God but the name of the Soul at the center by which all things are what they are, and so our existence is proof of his? We cannot think of ourselves and how our being is intertwined with his without awe and amazement."

—JOURNAL, 1832

Who or what is God to you? Do you agree with Emerson that God is "but the name of the Soul at the center by which all things are what they are"?

MAY 28

I believe that our own experience instructs us that the secret of Education lies in respecting the pupil. It is not for you to choose what he shall know, what he shall do. It is chosen and foreordained, and he only holds the key to his own secret. By your tampering and thwarting and too much governing he may be hindered from his end and kept out of his own. Respect the child. Wait and see the new product of Nature. Nature loves analogies, but not repetitions. Respect the child. Be not too much his parent. Trespass not on his solitude. But I hear the outcry which replies to this suggestion:—Would you verily throw up the reins of public and private discipline; would you leave the young child to the mad career of his own passions and whimsies, and call this anarchy a respect for the child's nature? I answer,—Respect the child, respect him to the end, but also respect yourself. Be the companion of his thought, the friend of his friendship, the lover of his virtue,—but no kinsman of his sin. Let him find you so true to yourself that you are the irreconcilable hater of his vice and the imperturbable slighter of his trifling.

—EDUCATION

Do you respect children, or do you try to mold them to your expectations? Do you fear that you will spoil them if you respect them?

There is no tax on the good of virtue; for that is the incoming of God himself, or absolute existence, without any comparative. Material good has its tax, and if it came without desert or sweat, has no root in me, and the next wind will blow it away. But all the good of nature is the soul's, and may be had, if paid for in nature's lawful coin, that is, by labor which the heart and the head allow. I no longer wish to meet a good I do not earn, for example, to find a pot of buried gold, knowing that it brings with it new burdens. I do not wish more external goods,— neither possessions, nor honors, nor powers, nor persons. The gain is apparent; the tax is certain. But there is no tax on the knowledge that the compensation exists, and that it is not desirable to dig up treasure. Herein I rejoice with a serene eternal peace.

—COMPENSATION

Do you believe, as Emerson does, that there is no price to be paid for spiritual goods, only material ones? What is a spiritual good to you?

Belief consists in accepting the affirmations of the soul; unbelief, in denying them. Some minds are incapable of skepticism. The doubts they profess to entertain are rather a civility or accommodation to the common discourse of their company. They may well give themselves leave to speculate, for they are secure of a return. Once admitted to the heaven of thought, they see no relapse into night, but infinite invitation on the other side. Heaven is within heaven, and sky over sky, and they are encompassed with divinities. Others there are to whom the heaven is brass, and it shuts down to the surface of the earth. It is a question of temperament, or of more or less immersion in nature. The last class must needs have a reflex or parasite faith; not a sight of realities, but an instinctive reliance on the seers and believers of realities. The manners and thoughts of believers astonish them and convince them that these have seen something which is hid from themselves. But their sensual habit would fix the believer to his last position, whilst he as inevitably advances; and presently the unbeliever, for love of belief, burns the believer.

—MONTAIGNE; OR, THE SKEPTIC

Are you incapable of skepticism, or do you think "the heaven is brass"? Is yours "a faith of realities" or "a reflex or parasite faith"?

The characteristic of heroism is its persistency. All men have wandering impulses, fits, and starts of generosity. But when you have chosen your part, abide by it, and do not weakly try to reconcile yourself with the world. The heroic cannot be the common, nor the common the heroic. Yet we have the weakness to expect the sympathy of people in those actions whose excellence is that they outrun sympathy, and appeal to a tardy justice. If you would serve your brother, because it is fit for you to serve him, do not take back your words when you find that prudent people do not commend you. Adhere to your own act, and congratulate yourself if you have done something strange and extravagant, and broken the monotony of a decorous age. It was a high counsel that I once heard given to a young person,—"Always do what you are afraid to do."

—HEROISM

How do you define heroism? Did you ever have the courage to do "something strange and extravagant"?

JUNE

Meditations

JUNE 1

Has the doctrine ever been fairly preached of man's moral nature? The whole world holds on to formal Christianity, and nobody teaches the essential truth, the heart of Christianity, for fear of shocking, etc. Every teacher, when once he finds himself insisting with all his might upon a great truth, turns up the ends of it at last with a cautious showing how it is agreeable to the life and teaching of Jesus—as if that was any recommendation. As if the blessedness of Jesus' life and teaching were not because they were agreeable to the truth. Well this cripples his teaching. It bereaves the truth he inculcates of more than half its force by representing it as something secondary that can't stand alone. The truth of truth consists in this, that it is self-evident, self-subsistent. It is light. You don't get a candle to see the sun rise.

—JOURNAL, 1832

What do you think is "the essential truth, the heart of Christianity"? Is what was true for Jesus true for you?

JUNE 2

We figure to ourselves Intellect as an ethereal sea, which ebbs and flows, which surges and washes hither and thither, carrying its whole virtue into every creek and inlet which it bathes. To this sea every human house has a water front. But this force, creating nature, visiting whom it will and withdrawing from whom it will, making day where it comes and leaving night when it departs, is no fee or property of mad or angel. It is as the light, public and entire to each, and on the same terms. What but thought deepens life, and makes us better than cow or cat? The grandeur of the impression the stars and heavenly bodies make on us is surely more valuable than our exact perception of a tub or table on the ground.

—Natural History of Intellect

Do you feel the ebb and flow of intellect? When was the last time you felt it surge?

JUNE 3

It is for want of self-culture that the superstition of Travelling, whose idols are Italy, England, Egypt, retains its fascination for all educated Americans....The soul is no traveller; the wise man stays at home, and when his necessities, his duties, on any occasion call him from his house, or into foreign lands, he is at home still, and shall make men sensible by the expression of his countenance, that he goes the missionary of wisdom and virtue, and visits cities and men like a sovereign, and not like an interloper or a valet....He carries ruins to ruins. Travelling is a fool's paradise.

—SELF-RELIANCE

Do you agree with Emerson that "travelling is a fool's paradise"? What do you suppose he means by that?

JUNE 4

These enchantments of Nature are medicinal, they sober and heal us. These are plain pleasures, kindly and native to us. We come to our own, and make friends with matter, which the ambitious chatter of the schools would persuade us to despise. We never can part with it; the mind loves its old home: as water to our thirst, so is the rock, the ground, to our eyes, and hands and feet. It is firm water: it is cold flame: what health, what affinity! Ever an old friend, ever like a dear friend and brother, when we chat affectedly with strangers, comes in this honest face, and takes a grave liberty with us, and shames us out of our nonsense. Cities give not the human sense room enough. We go out daily and nightly to feed the eyes on the horizon, and require so much scope, just as we need water for our bath.

—NATURE

Do you find nature to be medicinal and healing? How often do you experience it?

The religion which is to guide and satisfy the present and coming ages, whatever else it be, must be intellectual. The scientific mind must have a faith which is science. "There are two things," said Mahomet, "which I abhor, the learned in his infidelities, and the fool in his devotions." Our times are very impatient of both, and specially of the last. Let us have nothing now which is not its own evidence. There is surely enough for the heart and the imagination. Our books are full of generous biographies of saints, who knew not that they were such; of men and of women who lived for the benefit and healing of nature. But one fact I read in them all,—that, there is a religion which survives immutably all persons and fashions, and is worshipped and pronounced with emphasis again and again by some holy person;—and men, with their weak incapacity for principles, and their passion for persons, have run mad for the pronouncer, and forgot the religion.

—THE TENDENCIES AND DUTIES OF MEN OF THOUGHT

Is your faith grounded in experience or in the biographies of other people? What is the constant faith that transcends "all persons and fashions"?

JUNE 6

What are the best days in memory? Those in which we met a companion who was truly such. How sweet those hours when the day was not long enough to communicate and compare our intellectual jewels,—the favorite passages of each book, the proud anecdotes of our heroes, the delicious verses we had hoarded! What a motive had then our solitary days! How the countenance of our friend still left some light after he had gone! We remember the time when the best gift we could ask of fortune was to fall in with a valuable companion in a ship's cabin, or on a long journey in the old stage-coach, where, each passenger being forced to know every other, and other employments being out of question, conversation naturally flowed, people became rapidly acquainted, and, if well adapted, more intimate in a day than if they had been neighbors for years.

—CLUBS

Can you recall meaningful conversations you have had? With whom do you share and compare your "intellectual jewels"?

Our age is retrospective. It builds the sepulchers of the fathers. It writes biographies, histories, and criticism. The foregoing generations beheld God and nature face to face; we, through their eyes. Why should not we also enjoy an original relation to the universe? Why should not we have a poetry and philosophy of insight and not of tradition, and a religion by revelation to us, and not the history of theirs? Embosomed for a season in nature, whose floods of life stream around and through us, and invite us by the powers they supply, to action proportioned to nature, why should we grope among the dry bones of the past, or put the living generation into masquerade out of its faded wardrobe? The sun shines today also. There is more wool and flax in the fields. There are new lands, new men, new thoughts. Let us demand our own works and laws and worship.

—NATURE

Is revelation something from the past, or is there, as Emerson insists, revelation to be had today? What is the religion that is revealed to you?

JUNE 8

These are the voices which we hear in solitude, but they grow faint and inaudible as we enter into the world. Society everywhere is in conspiracy against the manhood of every one of its members. Society is a joint-stock company, in which the members agree, for the better securing of his bread to each shareholder, to surrender the liberty and culture of the eater. The virtue in most request is conformity. Self-reliance is its aversion. It loves not realities and creators, but names and customs. Whoso would be a man must be a nonconformist. He who would gather immortal palms must not be hindered by the name of goodness, but must explore if it be goodness. Nothing is at last sacred but the integrity of your own mind. Absolve you to yourself, and you shall have the suffrage of the world.

—Self-Reliance

Are you now or have you ever been a nonconformist? How difficult is it to be one? What price would one have to pay?

JUNE 9

How easily, if fate would suffer it, we might keep forever these beautiful limits, and adjust ourselves, once for all, to the perfect calculation of the kingdom of known cause and effect. In the street and in the newspapers, life appears so plain a business, that manly resolution and adherence to the multiplication-table through all weathers, will insure success. But ah! presently comes a day, or is it only a half-hour, with its angel-whispering,—which discomfits the conclusions of nations and of years! Tomorrow again, everything looks real and angular, the habitual standards are reinstated, common sense is as rare as genius,—is the basis of genius, and experience is hands and feet to every enterprise;—and yet, he who should do his business on this understanding, would be quickly bankrupt. Power keeps quite another road than the turnpikes of choice and will, namely, the subterranean and invisible tunnels and channels of life. . . . Life is a series of surprises, and would not be worth taking or keeping, if it were not. God delights to isolate us every day, and hide from us the past and the future. We would look about us, but with grand politeness he draws down before us an impenetrable screen of purest sky, and another behind us of purest sky. "You will not remember," he seems to say, "and you will not expect."

—EXPERIENCE

Is serendipity an important part of your spiritual life? What surprises has life visited on you?

JUNE 10

"It is not so in your experience," said Sampson Reed, "but is so in the other world." "Other world," I reply, "there is but one. Here or nowhere is the whole fact.". . . I see the unity of thought and of morals running through all animated nature. There is no difference of quality, but only of more and less. The animals all act with perfect good sense, act as a man would act, if his brain were cramped by their limitations. Life is one and not diverse: the life in us is the entrance of God into us: if he depart out of us, the dust he had enchanted moulders again, but he, the soul that built it, animates new forms, and carries the same energy to new work elsewhere; perhaps to purer, more un-obstructed action. This clay, which is momentarily animated, imagines it is for itself and would appropriate the generous tor-rents of power that stream through it for its own permanence and magnification. So, it becomes a wen, a goiter, a disease.

—NATURAL RELIGION

Do you agree that "life is one and not diverse"? Do you believe, as Emerson does, that we are diminished by a sense of independence and individualism?

JUNE 11

The chief good of life seems, this morning, to be born with a cheerful happy temper, and well adjusted to the tone of the human race: for then we feel ourselves in the harmony of things, and conscious of an infinite strength. He need not do anything. But if he is not well mixed and averaged, then he needs to achieve something, build a rail road, make a fortune, write an Iliad, as compensation to himself for his abnormal position, and as we pinch ourselves to know that we are awake.

—JOURNAL, 1847

Would you say that you are "well mixed and averaged"? Or do you think you need to compensate for your "abnormal position"?

JUNE 12

There is a tendency in things to right themselves, and the war or revolution or bankruptcy that shatters a rotten system, allows things to take a new and natural order. The sharpest evils are bent into that periodicity which makes the errors of planets, and the fevers and distempers of men, self-limiting. Nature is upheld by antagonism. Passions, resistance, danger, are educators. We acquire the strength we have overcome. Without war, no soldier; without enemies, no hero. The sun were insipid, if the universe were not opaque. And the glory of character is in affronting the horrors of depravity, to draw thence new nobilities of power: as Art lives and thrills in new use and combining of contrasts, and mining into the dark evermore for blacker pits of night. What would painter do, or what would poet or saint, but for crucifixions and hells? And evermore in the world is this marvellous balance of beauty and disgust, magnificence and rats.

—CONSIDERATIONS BY THE WAY

Is there a tendency in things to right themselves? Does creativity require conflict?

JUNE 13

Where do we find ourselves? In a series of which we do not know the extremes, and believe that it has none. We wake and find ourselves on a stair; there are stairs below us, which we seem to have ascended; there are stairs above us, many a one, which go upward and out of sight. But the Genius which, according to the old belief, stands at the door by which we enter, and gives us the lethe to drink, that we may tell no tales, mixed the cup too strongly, and we cannot shake off the lethargy now at noonday. Sleep lingers all our lifetime about our eyes, as night hovers all day in the boughs of the fir-tree. All things swim and glitter. Our life is not so much threatened as our perception. Ghostlike we glide through nature, and should not know our place again.... [I]t appears to us that we lack the affirmative principle, and though we have health and reason, yet we have no superfluity of spirit for new creation.... We have enough to live and bring the year about, but not an ounce to impart or to invest.... We are like millers on the lower levels of a stream, when the factories above them have exhausted the water.

—Experience

Have you ever felt dissociated from life and thought? Have you ever felt that you were sleep-walking through life?

The great art which religion teaches, is the art of conducting life well, not only in a view to future well-being, but in the very best manner, if there were no future state. Every serious man looks to religion for the supply of wants which he deeply feels. We want such views of life and duty as shall harmonize all we do and suffer;—as shall present us with motives worthy of our nature, and objects sufficient for our powers of action. We want principles which shall give the greatest strength to our social union, and the greatest efficacy to social action. We want principles which shall guide us in ever transaction of life; that shall attend us into the shop, and the factory; that shall make contracts, and project enterprises, and give gifts, and receive favours. We want principles that shall direct our education when we are young, and select our profession and control its exercise when we are mature; that shall assist us in forming our relationships, and connexions in life. We want principles that will bear the scrutiny of solitude, of doubt, of experience; that will fortify us against disaster; that will enable us to overcome every temptation, and every fear; and make us respectable and happy in ourselves when he have nothing and hope nothing on earth.

—SERMON 87

What do you look to religion for? Where do you find the principles you seek to guide your life by?

JUNE 15

Does Nature, my friend, never show you the wrong side of the tapestry? Never come to look dingy and shabby?...Or, on the other hand, do you find Nature always transcending and as good as new every day?... You have quite exhausted its power to please, and today you come into a new thought and lo! in an instant there stands the entire world converted suddenly into the cipher or exponent of that very thought, and chanting it in full chorus from every leaf and drop of water. It has been singing that song ever since the Creation in your deaf ears.

—JOURNAL, 1841

What song does nature sing to you? Does nature conform to your thoughts of it?

JUNE 16

I look for the hour when that supreme Beauty, which ravished the souls of those eastern men, and chiefly of those Hebrews, and through their lips spoke oracles to all time, shall speak in the West also.... I look for the new Teacher that shall follow so far those shining laws, that he shall see them come full circle; shall see their rounding complete grace; shall see the world to be the mirror of the soul; shall see the identity of the law of gravitation with purity of heart; and shall show that the Ought, that Duty, is one thing with Science, with Beauty, and with Joy.

—THE DIVINITY SCHOOL ADDRESS

Who are the teachers that speak in the West? Do you believe that duty is one with beauty, science, and joy?

Step by step we scale this mysterious ladder: the steps are actions; the new prospect is power. Every several result is threatened and judged by that which follows. Every one seems to be contradicted by the new; it is only limited by the new. The new statement is always hated by the old, and, to those dwelling in the old, comes like an abyss of skepticism. But the eye soon gets wonted to it, for the eye and it are effects of one cause; then its innocency and benefit appear, and presently, all its energy spent, it pales and dwindles before the revelation of the new hour. Fear not the new generalization. Does the fact look crass and material, threatening to degrade thy theory of spirit? Resist it not; it goes to refine and raise thy theory of matter just as much.

—Circles

Do you fear new generalizations? Do you find yourself growing more cautious and resistant with age?

JUNE 18

Bend to the persuasion which is flowing to you from every object in nature, to be its tongue to the heart of man, and to show the besotted world how passing fair is wisdom. Forewarned that the vice of the times and the country is an excessive pretension, let us seek the shade and find wisdom in neglect. Be content with a little light, so it be your own. Explore, and explore. Be neither chided nor flattered out of your position of perpetual inquiry. Neither dogmatize, nor accept another's dogmatism. Why should you renounce your right to traverse the star-lit deserts of truth, for the premature comforts of an acre, house, and barn? Truth also has its roof, and bed, and board. Make yourself necessary to the world, and mankind will give you bread, and if not store of it, yet such as shall not take away your property in all men's possessions, in all men's affections, in art, in nature, and in hope.

—LITERARY ETHICS

Can you be content with your own "little light"? Do you consider yourself a spiritual explorer?

JUNE 19

In the wood, God was manifest as he was not in the sermon. In the cathedralled larches the ground pine crept him, the thrush sang him, the robin complained him, the cat-bird mewed him, the anemone vibrated him, the wild apple bloomed him; the ants built their little Timbuctoo wide abroad; the wild grape budded; the rye was in the blade; high overhead, high over cloud the faint sharp-horned moon sailed steadily west through fleets of little clouds; the sheaves of the birch brightened into green below. The pines kneaded their aromatics in the sun. All prepared itself for the warm thunderdays of July.

—JOURNAL, 1838

Have you ever found God in the woods? What is the message of the sermon in the woods?

JUNE 20

Do what you know, and perception is converted into character, as islands and continents were built by invisible infusories, or, as these forest leaves absorb light, electricity, and volatile gases, and the gnarled oak to live a thousand years is the arrest and fixation of the most volatile and ethereal currents. The doctrine of this Supreme Presence is a cry of joy and exultation. Who shall dare think he has come late into nature, or has missed anything excellent in the past, who seeth the admirable stars of possibility, and the yet untouched continent of hope glittering with all its mountains in the vast West? I praise with wonder this great reality, which seems to drown all things in the deluge of its light. What man seeing this, can lose it from his thoughts, or entertain a meaner subject? The entrance of this into his mind seems to be the birth of man.

— THE METHOD OF NATURE

Do you rejoice in "the admirable stars of possibility"? What gives you grounds for hope, for joy and exultation?

JUNE 21

Dreams have a poetic integrity and truth. This limbo and dust-hole of thought is presided over by a certain reason, too. Their extravagance from nature is yet within a higher nature. They seem to us to suggest an abundance and fluency of thought not familiar to the waking experience. They pique us by independence of us, yet we know ourselves in this mad crowd, and owe to our dreams a kind of divination and wisdom. My dreams are not me; they are not Nature, or the Not-me: they are both. They have a double consciousness, at once sub- and ob-jective. We call the phantoms that rise, the creation of our fancy, but they act like mutineers, and fire on their commander; showing that every act, every thought, every cause, is bipolar, and in the act is contained the counteraction. If I strike, I am struck; if I chase, I am pursued.

—DEMONOLOGY

What credence do you give to dreams? Do your dreams "act like mutineers and fire on their commander"?

The soul is the perceiver and revealer of truth. We know truth when we see it, let skeptic and scoffer say what they choose. Foolish people ask you, when you have spoken what they do not wish to hear, "How do you know it is truth, and not an error of your own?" We know truth when we see it, from opinion, as we know when we are awake that we are awake.... In the book I read, the good thought returns to me, as every truth will, the image of the whole soul. To the bad thought which I find in it, the same soul becomes a discerning, separating sword, and lops it away. We are wiser than we know. If we will not interfere with our thought, but will act entirely, or see how the thing stands in God, we know the particular thing, and every thing, and every man. For the Maker of all things and all persons stands behind us, and casts his dread omniscience through us over things.

— THE OVER-SOUL

Do you know truth when you see it? How do you know it is the truth and not an error?

We say, the old forms of religion decay, and that a skepticism devastates the community. I do not think it can be cured or stayed by any modification of theologic creeds, much less by theologic discipline. The cure for false theology is mother wit. Forget your books and traditions, and obey your moral perceptions at this hour. That which is signified by the words "moral" and "spiritual," is a lasting essence, and, with whatever illusions we have loaded them, will certainly bring back the words, age after age, to their ancient meaning. I know no words that mean so much. In our definitions, we grope after the *spiritual* by describing it as invisible. The true meaning of *spiritual* is *real*; that law which executes itself, which works without means, and which cannot be conceived as not existing. . . . I find the omnipresence and the almightiness in the reaction of every atom in Nature. . . . Let us replace sentimentalism by realism, and dare to uncover those simple and terrible laws which, be they seen or unseen, pervade and govern.

— WORSHIP

What is your definition of the word spiritual*? Is an appreciation of spirituality necessary for the welfare of religion?*

JUNE 24

We owe to genius always the same debt, of lifting the curtain from the common, and showing us that divinities are sitting disguised in the seeming gang of gypsies and peddlers. In daily life, what distinguishes the master is the using those materials he has, instead of looking about for what are more renowned, or what others have used well.... Do not refuse the employment which the hour brings you, for one more ambitious. The highest heaven of wisdom is alike near from every point, and thou must find it, if at all, by methods native to thyself alone.

—WORKS AND DAYS

Have you experienced the divine disguised as a gypsy or peddler? How have you found "the highest heaven of wisdom" in your life?

JUNE 25

We spend our incomes for paint and paper, for a hundred trifles, I know not what, and not for the things of a man. Our expense is almost all for conformity.... Why needs any man be rich? Why must he have horses, fine garments, handsome apartments, access to public houses, and places of amusement? Only for want of thought. Give his mind a new image, and he flees into a solitary garden or garret to enjoy it, and is richer with that dream, than the fee of a county could make him. But we are first thoughtless, and then find that we are moneyless. We are first sensual, and then must be rich. We dare not trust our wit for making our house pleasant to our friend, and so we buy ice-creams. He is accustomed to carpets, and we have not sufficient character to put floor-cloths out of his mind whilst he stays in the house, and so we pile the floor with carpets. Let the house rather be a temple . . . , formidable and holy to all, which none but a Spartan may enter or so much as behold. As soon as there is faith, as soon as there is society, comfits and cushions will be left to slaves. Expense will be inventive and heroic. We shall eat hard and lie hard, we shall dwell like the ancient Romans in narrow tenements, whilst our public edifices, like theirs, will be worthy for their proportion of the landscape in which we set them, for conversation, for art, for music, for worship. We shall be rich to great purposes; poor only for selfish ones. It is better to go without, than to have them at too great a cost.

—MAN THE REFORMER

Do you spend for conformity or for genius? What does economy mean to you?

JUNE 26

But real action is in silent moments. The epochs of our life are not in the visible facts of our choice of a calling, our marriage, our acquisition of an office, and the like, but in a silent thought by the way-side as we walk; in a thought which revises our entire manner of life, and says,—"Thus hast thou done, but it were better thus." And all our after years, like menials, serve and wait on this, and, according to their ability, execute its will. This revisal or correction is a constant force, which, as a tendency, reaches through our lifetime. The object of the man, the aim of these moments, is to make daylight shine through him, to suffer the law to traverse his whole being without obstruction, so that, on what point soever of his doing your eye falls, it shall report truly of his character, whether it be his diet, his house, his religious forms, his society, his mirth, his vote, his opposition. Now he is not homogeneous, but heterogeneous, and the ray does not traverse; there are no thorough lights: but the eye of the beholder is puzzled, detecting many unlike tendencies, and a life not yet at one.

—Spiritual Laws

Have you entertained "a silent thought by the way-side" recently? Is your aim in life "to make daylight shine through you"?

Success goes thus invariably with a certain plus or positive power: an ounce of power must balance an ounce of weight. And, though a man cannot return into his mother's womb, and be born with new amounts of vivacity, yet there are two economies, which are the best succedanea which the case admits. The first is, the stopping off decisively our miscellaneous activity, and concentrating our force on one or a few points; as the gardener, by severe pruning, forces the sap of the tree into one or two vigorous limbs, instead of suffering it to spindle into a sheaf of twigs.... The second substitute for temperament is drill, the power of use and routine.... In chemistry, the galvanic stream, slow, but continuous, is equal in power to the electric spark, and is, in our arts, a better agent. So in human action, against the spasm of energy, we offset the continuity of drill. We spread the same amount of force over much time, instead of condensing it into a moment.

—POWER

What does your spiritual practice consist of? In what ways do you concentrate your force? What part do drill and routine play?

JUNE 28

We cannot part with our friends. We cannot let our angels go. We do not see that they only go out, that archangels may come in. We are idolaters of the old. We do not believe in the riches of the soul, in its proper eternity and omnipresence. We do not believe there is any force in today to rival or recreate that beautiful yesterday. We linger in the ruins of the old tent, where once we had bread and shelter and organs, nor believe that the spirit can feed, cover, and nerve us again. We cannot again find aught so dear, so sweet, so graceful. But we sit and weep in vain. The voice of the Almighty saith, "Up and onward for evermore!" We cannot stay amid the ruins. Neither will we rely on the new; and so we walk ever with reverted eyes, like those monsters who look backwards.

—COMPENSATION

Do you agree that people, as a rule, do not believe in the riches of the soul? Why are we unwilling to rely on the new?

JUNE 29

Goethe teaches courage, and the equivalence of all times; that the disadvantages of any epoch exist only to the faint-hearted. Genius hovers with his sunshine and music close by the darkest and deafest eras. No mortgage, no attainder, will hold on men or hours. The world is young: the former great men call to us affectionately. We too must write Bibles, to unite again the heavens and the earthly world. The secret of genius is to suffer no fiction to exist for us; to realize all that we know; in the high refinement of modern life, in arts, in sciences, in books, in men, to exact good faith, reality and a purpose; and first, last, midst and without end, to honor every truth by use.

—GOETHE; OR, THE WRITER

Where is the genius in our era? Who is writing Bibles today?

JUNE 30

When I remember the twofold cord, then fourfold and go a little back a thousand and a millionfold cord of which my being and every man's being consists; that I am an aggregate of infinitesimal parts and that every minutest streamlet that has flowed to me is represented in that man which I am, so that if everyone should claim his part in me I should be instantaneously diffused through the creation and individually decease, then I say if I am but an alms of All, and live but by the Charity of innumerable others, there is no peculiar propriety in wrapping my cloak about me and hiding the ray that my taper may emit. What is a man but a Congress of nations? Just suppose for one moment to appear before him the whole host of his ancestors. All have vanished; he—the insulated result of all that character, activity, sympathy, antagonism working for ages in all corners of the earth—alone remains. Such is his origin; well was his nurture less compound. Who and what has not contributed something to make him that he is? Art, science, institutions, black men, white men, the vices and virtues of all people, the gallows, the church, the shop, poets, nature, joy, and fear, all help all teach him. Every fairy brings a gift.

—JOURNAL, 1834

What are some of the streamlets that have flowed into you?
Who and what have contributed to make you what you are?

JULY

Meditations

JULY 1

But life is good only when it is magical and musical, a perfect timing and consent, and when we do not anatomize it. You must treat the days respectfully, you must be a day yourself, and not interrogate it like a college professor. The world is enigmatical,—everything said, and everything known or done,—and must not be taken literally, but genially. We must be at the top of our condition to understand anything rightly. You must hear the bird's song without attempting to render it into nouns and verbs. Cannot we be a little abstemious and obedient? Cannot we let the morning be?

—WORKS AND DAYS

How do you treat the days? What do you do to be ready "to understand anything rightly"?

JULY 2

We must not affect as all mankind do, to know all things and to have quite finished and done God and Heaven. We must come back to our real initial state and see and own that we have yet beheld but the first ray of Being. In strict speech it seems fittest to say, *I Become* rather than *I am*. I am a *Becoming*. So do I less sever or divide the One. I am now nothing but a prophesy of that I shall be. To me sing and chant sun and stars and persons; they all manifest to me my far off rights. They foreshadow or they are the first ripples and wavelets of that vast inundation of the All which is beyond and which I tend and labor to be.

—JOURNAL, 1838

Can we ever "know it all and be quite done with God and Heaven"? Do nature and human beings represent a process and never a completion?

JULY 3

To Be is the unsolved, unsolvable wonder. To Be, in its two connections of inward and outward, the mind and Nature. The wonder subsists, and age, though of eternity, could not approach a solution. But the suggestion is always returning, that hidden source publishing at once our being and that it is the source of outward Nature. Who are we, and what is Nature, have one answer in the life that rushes into us. In my thought I seem to stand on the bank of a river and watch the endless flow of the stream, floating objects of all shapes, colors and natures; nor can I much detain them as they pass, except by running beside them a little way along the bank. But whence they come or whither they go is not told me. Only I have a suspicion that, as geologists say every river makes its own valley, so does this mystic stream. It makes its valley, makes its banks and makes perhaps the observer too. Who has found the boundaries of human intelligence? Who has made a chart of its channel, or approached the fountain of this wonderful Nile? I am of the oldest religion. Leaving aside the question which was prior, egg or bird, I believe the mind is the creator of the world, and is ever creating; . . . that mind makes the senses it sees with; that the genius of man is a continuation of the power that made him and that has not done making him.

—NATURAL HISTORY OF INTELLECT

Is the mind "the creator of the world"? Have you ever had the experience of standing on the bank of the river of life and watching its endless flow? What was that like?

JULY 4

The theory of our government is Liberty. The thought and experience of Europe had got thus far, a century ago, to believe, that, as soon as favorable circumstances permitted, the experiment of self-government should be made. America afforded the circumstances, and the new order began. All the mind in America was possessed by that idea. The Declaration of Independence, the Constitution of the States; the parties; the newspapers, the songs, *The Star-spangled Banner*...the very manners of the Americans, all showed them as the receivers and propagandists of this lesson to the world....It was not a sect, it was not a private opinion, but a gradual and irresistible growth of the human mind. That is the meaning of our national pride. That is at the bottom of all of our brag about the star-spangled banner. It is a noble office. For liberty is a very serious thing. It is the severest test by which a government can be tried. All history goes to show, that it is the measure of all national success. Religion, arts, science, material production are as is the degree of liberty....Most unhappily, this universally accepted duty and feeling have been antagonized by the calamity of southern slavery. And that institution, in its perpetual encroachment, has had...the art so to league itself with the government, as to check and pervert the natural sentiment of the people by their respect for law and statute. And this country exhibits an abject regard to the forms, whilst we are swindled out of the liberty.

— AMERICAN SLAVERY

Can liberty ever coexist with oppression? Have we completely realized the notion of liberty in this country? Do our government, society, and institutions pass the test of liberty?

JULY 5

Why should we make it a point with our false modesty to disparage that man we are, and that form of being assigned to us? A good man is contented. I love and honor Epaminondas, but I do not wish to be Epaminondas. I hold it more just to love the world of this hour, than the world of his hour.... Heaven is large, and affords space for all modes of love and fortitude. Why should we be busybodies and superserviceable? Action and inaction are alike to the true. One piece of the tree is cut for a weathercock, and one for the sleeper of a bridge; the virtue of the wood is apparent in both. I desire not to disgrace the soul. The fact that I am here certainly shows me that the soul had need of an organ here. Shall I not assume the post? Shall I skulk and dodge and duck with my unseasonable apologies and vain modesty, and imagine my being here impertinent? less pertinent than Epaminondas or Homer being there? and that the soul did not know its own needs? Besides, without any reasoning on the matter, I have no discontent. The good soul nourishes me, and unlocks new magazines of power and enjoyment to me every day. I will not meanly decline the immensity of good, because I have heard that it has come to others in another shape.

—SPIRITUAL LAWS

Have you ever felt that you were assuming the post of a "soul that needed an organ here"? What does it mean to "desire not to disgrace the soul"?

All good conversation, manners, and action, come from a spontaneity which forgets usages, and makes the moment great. Nature hates calculators; her methods are saltatory and impulsive. Man lives by pulses; our organic movements are such; and the chemical and ethereal agents are undulatory and alternate; and the mind goes antagonizing on, and never prospers but by fits. We thrive by casualties. Our chief experiences have been casual. The most attractive class of people are those who are powerful obliquely, and not by the direct stroke: men of genius, but not yet accredited: one gets the cheer of their light, without paying too great a tax. Theirs is the beauty of the bird, or the morning light, and not of art. In the thought of genius there is always a surprise; and the moral sentiment is well called "the newness," for it is never other; as new to the oldest intelligence as to the young child.... The art of life has a pudency, and will not be exposed. Every man is an impossibility, until he is born; every thing impossible, until we see a success.... I would gladly be moral, and keep due metes and bounds, which I dearly love, and allow the most to the will of man, but I have set my heart on honesty... and I can see nothing at last, in success or failure, than more or less of vital force supplied from the Eternal. The results of life are uncalculated and uncalculable. The years teach much which the days never know. The persons who compose our company, converse, and come and go, and design and execute many things, and somewhat comes of it all, but an unlooked for result. The individual is always mistaken.

—EXPERIENCE

Are there people you admire for their spontaneity and unpredictability? What have the years taught you?

JULY 7

Our recent culture has been in natural science. We have learned the manners of the sun and of the moon, of the rivers and the rains, of the mineral and elemental kingdoms, of plants and animals. Man has learned to weigh the sun, and its weight neither loses nor gains. The path of a star, the moment of an eclipse, can be determined to the fraction of a second. Well, to him the book of history, the book of love, the lures of passion, and the commandments of duty are opened: and the next lesson taught, is, the continuation of the inflexible law of matter into the subtle kingdom of will, and of thought; that, if, in sidereal ages, gravity and projection keep their craft, and the ball never loses its way in its wild path through space,—a secreter gravitation, a secreter projection, rule not less tyrannically in human history, and keep the balance of power from age to age unbroken. For, though the new element of freedom and an individual has been admitted, yet the primordial atoms are prefigured and predetermined to moral issues, are in search of justice, and ultimate right is done. Religion or worship is the attitude of those who see this unity, intimacy, and sincerity; who see that, against all appearances, the nature of things works for truth and right forever.

—WORSHIP

Are there moral laws as well as natural laws? Is there a relation between the two, such that "the primordial atoms are prefigured and predetermined to moral issues"?

JULY 8

What is life, but the angle of vision? A man is measured by the angle at which he looks at objects. What is life—but what a man is thinking of all day? This is his fate and his employer. The brain is the man. The eyes outrun the feet, and go where feet and hands will never come; yet it is very certain that the rest of the man will follow his head. The history of intellect will be the best of all chronicles, and quite supercede them. 'Tis true there are quick bounds to our knowledge, but we cannot therefore undervalue what we know. As gems among pebbles catch the savage eye brooding over their mysterious luster, so over truths we hover and muse, assuring ourselves of their high import. We go on hiving thoughts from year to year, without any precise object, but only from an instinct of their intrinsic worth, and in the belief that they are also to have a new value to us one day as our history opens.

—THE POWERS AND LAWS OF THOUGHT

What is your "angle of vision" on life? What do you think about all day? What does that say about your life and what you consider important?

JULY 9

Wherever is life, wherever is God, there the Universe evolves itself as from a centre to its boundless irradiation. Whosoever therefore apprehends the infinite, and every man can, brings all worth and significance into that spot of space where he stands though it be a ditch, a potato-field, a work-bench; or, more properly into that state of thought in which he is, whether it be the making of a statue or designing a church.... Therefore it is in the option of every generous spirit to denominate that place in which he now is, his Rome, his world.... And therefore also is it true that every good sentence seems to imply all truth.

—JOURNAL, 1834

What is your Rome, your world? What do you bring to that place where you stand?

JULY 10

Crossing a bare common, in snow puddles, at twilight, under a clouded sky, without having in my thoughts any occurrence of special good fortune, I have enjoyed a perfect exhilaration. I am glad to the brink of fear. In the woods too, a man casts off his years, as the snake its slough, and at what period soever of life, is always a child. In the woods, is perpetual youth. Within these plantations of God, a decorum and sanctity reign, a perennial festival is dressed, and the guest sees not how he should tire of them in a thousand years. In the woods, we return to reason and faith. There I feel that nothing can befall me in life,—no disgrace, no calamity (leaving me my eyes) which nature cannot repair. Standing on the bare ground,—my head bathed by the blithe air and uplifted into infinite space,— all mean egotism vanishes. I become a transparent eyeball; I am nothing; I see all; the currents of Universal Being circulate through me; I am part or particle of God.

—NATURE

Can you recall a mystical experience you have had? What did you learn from it? How did you feel?

JULY 11

We cannot describe the natural history of the soul, but we know that it is divine. I cannot tell if these wonderful qualities which house today in this mortal frame, shall ever reassemble in equal activity in a similar frame, or whether they have before had a natural history like that of this body you see before you; but this one thing I know, that these qualities did not now begin to exist, cannot be sick with my sickness, nor buried in any grave; but that they circulate through the Universe: before the world was, they were. Nothing can bar them out, or shut them in, but they penetrate the ocean and land, space and time, form and essence, and hold the key to universal nature. I draw from this faith courage and hope. All things are known to the soul. It is not to be surprised by any communication. Nothing can be greater than it. Let those fear and those fawn who will. The soul is in her native realm, and it is wider than space, older than time, rich as love.

—THE METHOD OF NATURE

Is the soul divine? Does it connect you to "universal nature"?

The compensations of calamity are made apparent to the understanding also, after long intervals of time. A fever, a mutilation, a cruel disappointment, a loss of wealth, a loss of friends, seems at the moment unpaid loss, and unpayable. But the sure years reveal the deep remedial force that underlies all facts. The death of a dear friend, wife, brother, lover, which seemed nothing but privation, somewhat later assumes the aspect of a guide or genius; for it commonly operates revolutions in our way of life, terminates an epoch of infancy or of youth which was waiting to be closed, breaks up a wonted occupation, or a household, or style of living, and allows the formation of new ones more friendly to the growth of character. It permits or constrains the formation of new acquaintances, and the reception of new influences that prove of the first importance to the next years; and the man or woman who would have remained a sunny garden-flower, with no room for its roots and too much sunshine for its head, by the falling of the walls and the neglect of the gardener is made the banian of the forest, yielding shade and fruit to wide neighborhoods of men.

—COMPENSATION

Have your experiences of pain and loss engendered revolutions in your way of life? Can you think of any compensations of calamity?

JULY 13

We do not know today whether we are busy or idle. In times when we thought ourselves indolent, we have afterwards discovered, that much was accomplished, and much was begun in us. All our days are so unprofitable while they pass, that 'tis wonderful where or when we ever got anything of this which we call wisdom, poetry, virtue. We never got it on any dated calendar day. Some heavenly days must have been intercalated somewhere.... Every ship is a romantic object, except that we sail in. Embark, and the romance quits our vessel, and hangs on every other sail in the horizon. Our life looks trivial, and we shun to record it.... Every roof is agreeable to the eye, until it is lifted; then we find tragedy and moaning women, and hard-eyed husbands, and deluges of lethe, and the men ask, 'What's the news?' as if the old were so bad. How many individuals can we count in society? how many actions? how many opinions? So much of our time is preparation, so much is routine, and so much retrospect, that the pith of each man's genius contracts itself to a very few hours.

—Experience

Have you ever felt that your life was trivial? Have you felt that your life is merely routine and retrospective?

JULY 14

The one prudence in life is concentration; the one evil is dissipation: and it makes no difference whether our dissipations are course or fine; property and its cares, friends and a sociable habit, or politics, or music, or feasting. Everything is good which takes away one plaything and delusion more, and drives us home to add one stroke of faithful work. Friends, books, pictures, lower duties, talents, flatteries, hopes,—all are distractions which cause oscillations in our giddy balloon, and make a good poise and a straight course impossible. You must elect your work; you shall take what your brain can, and drop all the rest. Only so, can that amount of vital force accumulate, which can make the step from knowing to doing. No matter how much faculty of idle seeing a man has, the step from knowing to doing is rarely taken....Concentration is the secret of strength in politics, in war, in trade, in short in all management of human affairs.

— POWER

Are you able to concentrate your force and attention? Are you easily distracted? What distracts you?

JULY 15

Here are we new men on this old-new, eternal, yet flowing existence, learning thus the lessons which patriarch, and saint, and hero have learned in their day and crisis. The earth has lost no virtues, the sun no beams; seed time and harvest punctually return. And all natures not less impress their secondary and interior meaning on the soul, and speak to the imagination, and admonish life. There are in many parts of Europe old churches which still show in their massive walls that they were once Greek and Roman temples of Jove and Diana, and I doubt not that good hearts with much the same religious aspiration worshipped in the older and in the later ceremonial. But, here is the same round floor of earth; the same blue hollow of sky has offered to all the succession of tribes of men for many thousand years the same simple, penetrating thoughts—the same inquiries, the same duties, the new gifts, and curiosity and awe—before the immense benefactor who works the miracle of the universe. And still, in all the changes of race and condition, in all the varieties and pretension of teaching, the same livelong convictions of duty recur. Justice, Courage, Truth, and Charity, have their old majesty. The eye is still dazzled by the same outsides; the Reason still penetrates to the simplicity of principles, to the perfect compensation.

—NATURAL RELIGION

We have "the same inquiries, the same duties" as our forebears. We have "new gifts, and curiosity and awe." When will we have our own religion? What will it consist of?

JULY 16

Before tea I counted not myself worth a brass farthing, and now I am filled with thoughts and pleasures and am as strong and infinite as an angel. So when one of these days I see this body going to ruin like an old cottage, I will remember that after the ruin the resurrection is sure.... The principle of repairs is in us the remedial principle. Everybody perceives greatest contrasts in his own spirit and powers. Today he is not worth a brown cent—tomorrow he is better than a million. He kicks at riches and could be honoured and happy with nothing but arrowroot and balm tea. This we call being in good or bad spirits. It is only in the bad fit, that we doubt and deny and do ill, and we know well at that time that sorrow will come for the bad action; and sorrow is repairs, and belief in the powers and perpetuity of man will return, and shall be magnified by trust in God. When, therefore, I doubt and sin, I will look up at the moon, and, remembering that its errors are all periodical, I will anticipate the return of my own spirits and faith.

—JOURNAL, 1832

Do you believe there is a "principle of repairs" that assuages our doubts and sins? Have you experienced it?

JULY 17

In this glorious summer day, I have taken a turn in my woods. How gaily the wind practices his graces there and every tree and all the woods bow with gentlest yet majestic elegance. And the pine shakes out its pollen for the benefit of the next century. There I feel the newness and prerogative of me and of today. I would say to the young scholar: Permit none to invade your mind. Live with God alone. See how the spirit does execute every presentiment in some gigantic fact. What else is Egypt, Greece, Rome, England, France, St. Helena; what else are churches, and empires, and literature?... Say to such, you are greatly obliged to them as you are to all the History, to the pyramids, and the Authors, but now are we here, now our day is come, we have been born out of the Eternal silence and now will we live, live for ourselves and not as the pallbearers of a funeral but as the upholders and creators of an age.... Now we are come and will put our own interpretation on things and moreover our own things for interpretation.

—JOURNAL, 1838

Does nature inspire your creativity? Do we live for ourselves or "as the pallbearers" of the past?

JULY 18

We are to revise the whole of our social structure, the state, the school, religion, marriage, trade, science, and explore their foundations in our own nature; we are to see that the world not only fitted the former men, but fits us, and to clear ourselves of every usage which has not its roots in our own mind. What is a man born for but to be a Reformer, a Remaker of what man has made; a renouncer of lies; a restorer of truth and good, imitating that great Nature which embosoms us all, and which sleeps no moment on an old past, but every hour repairs herself, yielding us every morning a new day, and with every pulsation a new life? Let him renounce everything which is not true to him, and put all his practices back on their first thoughts, and do nothing for which he has not the whole world for his reason. If there are inconveniences, and what is called ruin in the way, because we have so enervated and maimed ourselves, yet it would be like dying of perfumes to sink in the effort to re-attach the deeds of every day to the holy and mysterious recesses of life.

—MAN THE REFORMER

Do you consider yourself a reformer? What would you reform if you could, and how would you reform it?

Insist on yourself; never imitate. Your own gift you can present every moment with the cumulative force of a whole life's cultivation; but of the adopted talent of another, you have only an extemporaneous, half possession. That which each can do best, none but his Maker can teach him. No man yet knows what it is, nor can, until that person has exhibited it. Where is the master who could have taught Shakespeare? Where is the master who could have instructed Franklin, or Washington, or Bacon, or Newton? Every great man is unique. The Scipionism of Scipio is precisely that part he could not borrow. Shakespeare will never be made by the study of Shakespeare. Do that which is assigned you, and you cannot hope too much or dare too much.

—SELF-RELIANCE

What is it that none but you can do? What do you think is "that which is assigned you"?

Our moods do not believe in each other. Today I am full of thoughts, and can write what I please. I see no reason why I should not have the same thought, the same power of expression, tomorrow. What I write, whilst I write it, seems the most natural thing in the world; but yesterday I saw a dreary vacuity in this direction in which now I see so much; and a month hence, I doubt not, I shall wonder who he was that wrote so many continuous pages. Alas for this infirm faith, this will not strenuous, this vast ebb of a vast flow! I am God in nature; I am a weed by the wall.

—CIRCLES

Are there times when you doubt your own power and productivity? Is there a steady accumulation of "continuous pages" in your life?

JULY 21

To me . . . the question of the times resolved itself into a practical question of the conduct of life. How shall I live? We are incompetent to solve the times. Our geometry cannot span the huge orbits of the prevailing ideas, behold their return, and reconcile their opposition. We can only obey our own polarity. 'Tis fine for us to speculate and elect our course, if we must accept an irresistible dictation. In our first steps to gain our wishes, we come upon immovable limitations. We are fired with the hope to reform men. After many experiments, we find that we must begin earlier,—at school. But the boys and girls are not docile; we can make nothing of them. We decide that they are not of good stock. We must begin our reform earlier still,—at generation: that is to say, there is Fate, or laws of the world. But if there be irresistible dictation, this dictation understands itself. If we must accept Fate, we are not less compelled to affirm liberty, the significance of the individual, the grandeur of duty, the power of character. This is true, and that other is true. But our geometry cannot span these extreme points, and reconcile them. What to do? . . . We are sure, that, though we know not how, necessity does comport with liberty, the individual with the world, my polarity with the spirit of the times.

—FATE

How shall you live? How do you resolve the antagonism between freedom and fate?

JULY 22

I wish to enforce the doctrine that a man should trust himself; should have a perfect confidence that there is no defect or inferiority in his nature; that when he discovers in himself different powers, or opinions, or manners, from others whom he loves and respects, he should not think of himself in that degree inferior, but only different; and that for every defect there is some compensation provided in his system; and that wherever there is manifest imperfection in his character, it springs from his own neglect to cultivate some part of his mind. I am afraid of this great tendency to uniformity of action and conversation among men. I am afraid of the great evil done to so sacred a property as a man's own soul by an imitation arising out of an unthinkable admiration of others. I believe God gave to every man the germ of a peculiar character. The ends of action are the same, but the means and the manner are infinitely various. As every man occupies a position in some respects singular, every man has probably thoughts that never entered the mind of any other man.

—SERMON 90

---

*Do you trust yourself? Do you have confidence that there is
"no defect or deformity" in your nature? Do you look too
much to others for your own answers and opinions?*

I would not have any superstition about solitude. Let the youth study the uses of solitude and of society. Let him use both, not serve either. The reason why an ingenious soul shuns society, is to the end of finding society. It repudiates the false, out of love of the true. You can very soon learn all that society can teach you for one while. Its foolish routine, an indefinite multiplication of balls, concerts, rides, theaters, can teach you no more than a few can. Then accept the hint of shame, of spiritual emptiness and waste, which true nature gives you, and retire, and hide; lock the door; shut the shutters; then welcome falls the imprisoning rain,—dear hermitage of nature. Re-collect the spirits. Have solitary prayer and praise. Digest and correct the past experience; and blend it with the new and divine life.

—LITERARY ETHICS

How do you make use of your times of solitude? Can you balance your need for solitude with your need for society?

JULY 24

For this I was born and came into the world to deliver the self of myself to the Universe from the Universe; to do a certain benefit which Nature could not forego, nor I be discharged from rendering, and then immerge again into the holy silence and eternity, out of which as a man I arose. God is rich and many more men than I, he harbors in his bosom, biding their time and the needs and the beauty of all. Or, when I wish, it is permitted me to say, these hands, this body, this history of Waldo Emerson are profane and wearisome, but I, I descend not to mix myself with that or with any man. Above his life, above all creatures I flow down forever a sea of benefit into races of individuals. Nor can the stream ever roll backward or the sin or death of a man taint the immutable energy which distributes itself into men as the sun into rays of the sea into drops.

—JOURNAL, 1841

What do you think you were born into the world to do? Do you have a destiny to fulfill?

JULY 25

The history of man is a series of conspiracies to win from Nature some advantage without paying for it. It is curious to see what grand powers we have a hint of and are mad to grasp, yet how slow Heaven is to trust us with such edge-tools. "All that frees talent without increasing self-command is noxious."... A new or private language, used to serve only low or political purposes...; the steam battery, so fatal as to put an end to war by the threat of universal murder; the desired discovery of the guided balloon, are of this kind. Tramps are troublesome enough in the city and in the highways, but tramps flying through the air and descending on the lonely traveler or the lonely farmer's house or the bank-messenger in the country, can well be spared. Men are not fit to be trusted with these talismans. Before we acquire great power we must acquire wisdom to use it well.

— DEMONOLOGY

Are we trying to win some advantage from nature without paying for it? Has wisdom preceded the use of our tools?

If now in this connection of discourse, we should venture on laying down the first obvious rules of life, I will not here repeat the first rule of economy, already propounded once and again, that every man shall maintain himself—but I will say, get health. No labor, pains, temperance, poverty, nor exercise, that can gain it, must be grudged. For sickness is a cannibal which eats up all the life and youth it can lay hold of, and absorbs its own sons and daughters. . . . And the best part of health is fine disposition. It is more essential than talent, even in the works of talent. Nothing will supply the want of sunshine to peaches, and, to make knowledge valuable, you must have the cheerfulness of wisdom. Whenever you are sincerely pleased, you are nourished. The joy of the spirit indicates its strength.

—CONSIDERATIONS BY THE WAY

Are you a cheerful person? What do you do to "get health"?

On my saying, What have I to do with the sacredness of traditions, if I live wholly from within? my friend suggested,—"But these impulses may be from below, not from above." I replied, "They do not seem to me to be such; but if I am the Devil's child, I will live then from the Devil." No law can be sacred to me but that of my nature. Good and bad are but names very readily transferable to that or this; the only right is what is after my constitution, the only wrong what is against it. A man is to carry himself in the presence of all opposition, as if every thing were titular and ephemeral but he. I am ashamed to think how easily we capitulate to badges and names, to large societies and dead institutions.

—Self-Reliance

Do your beliefs come from traditions or "wholly from within"? Have you been told your "impulses may be from below, not from above"?

JULY 28

We distinguish the announcements of the soul, its manifestations of its own nature, by the term *Revelation*. These are always attended by the emotion of the sublime. For this communication is an influx of the Divine mind into our mind. It is an ebb of the individual rivulet before the flowing surges of the sea of life. Every distinct apprehension of this central commandment agitates men with awe and delight.... Every moment when the individual feels himself invaded by it is memorable. By the necessity of our constitution, a certain enthusiasm attends the individual's consciousness of that divine presence. The character and duration of this enthusiasm varies with the state of the individual, from an ecstasy and trance and prophetic inspiration,— which is its rarer appearance,—to the faintest glow of virtuous emotion, in which form it warms, like our household fires, all the families and associations of men, and makes society possible.

— THE OVER-SOUL

Have you ever experienced a revelation? Was it in the form of an ecstatic trance, the faint "glow of virtuous emotion," or something in between?

JULY 29

My house stands in low land, with limited outlook, and on the skirt of the village. But I go with my friend to the shore of our little river, and with one stroke of the paddle, I leave...the world of villages and personalities behind, and pass into a delicate realm of sunset and moonlight, too bright almost for spotted man to enter without novitiate and probation. We penetrate bodily this incredible beauty; we dip our hands in this painted element: our eyes are bathed in these lights and forms. A holiday,...the proudest, most heart-rejoicing festival that valor and beauty, power and taste, ever decked and enjoyed, establishes itself on the instant. These sunset clouds, these delicately emerging stars, with their private and ineffable glances, signify it and proffer it. I am taught the poorness of our invention, the ugliness of towns and palaces....I am over-instructed for my return. Henceforth I shall be hard to please. I cannot go back to toys. I am grown expensive and sophisticated. I can no longer live without elegance....He who knows the most, he who knows what sweets and virtues are in the ground, the waters, the plants, the heavens and how to come at these enchantments, is the rich and royal man.

—NATURE

After a sojourn in nature, do you find it difficult to "go back to toys"? How are you made rich by your experience of nature?

JULY 30

He must embrace solitude as a bride. He must have his glees and his glooms alone. His own estimate must be measure enough, his own praise reward enough for him. And why must the student be solitary and silent? That he may become acquainted with his thoughts. If he pines in a lonely place, hankering for the crowd, for display, he is not in the lonely place; his heart is in the market; he does not see; he does not hear; he does not think. But go cherish your soul; expel companions; set your habits to a life of solitude; then, will the faculties rise fair and full within, like forest trees and field flowers; you will have results, which, when you meet your fellow-men, you can communicate, and they will gladly receive. Do not go into solitude only that you may presently come into public. Such solitude denies itself; is public and stale. The public can get public experience, but they wish the scholar to replace to them those private, sincere, divine experiences of which they have been defrauded by dwelling in the street.

— LITERARY ETHICS

Do you "embrace solitude as a bride"? What kinds of thoughts come to you in solitude?

What we do and suffer is in moments, but the cause of right for which we labor, never dies, works in long periods, can afford many checks, gains by our defeats, and will know how to compensate our extremest sacrifice. Wrath and petulance may have their short success, but they quickly reach their brief date, and decompose, whilst the massive might of ideas is irresistible at last. Whence does this knowledge come? Where is the source of power? The soul of God is poured into the world through the thoughts of men. As cloud on cloud, as snow on snow, as the bird on the air, and the planet rests on space in its flight, so do nations of men and their institutions rest on thoughts.

My point is, that the movement of the whole machine, the motive force of life, and of every particular life, is moral. The world stands on our thoughts, and not on iron or cotton; and the iron of iron, the fire of fire, the ether and source of all the elements, is moral force. It is a fagot of laws, and that band which ties them together is Unity, is Universal Good, saturating all the laws with one being and aim, so that each law translates the other; is only the same Spirit applied to new departments that, if we should really come down to atoms, of which men believed that the universe is composed, we should not find little cubes or atoms at all, but only spherules of force, a fagot of forces, a series of currents in which all things are forced to run;—a series of threads, on which men, and animals, and plants, and brute matter are strung as beads;—those forces only exist.

— PERPETUAL FORCES

Do you believe that you will be compensated your defeats for in the long run? Is there a cause for which you are willing to work without seeing the results in your lifetime?

AUGUST

Meditations

There is in every man a determination of character to a peculiar end, counteracted often by unfavorable fortune, but more apparent the more one is left at liberty. This is called his genius, or his nature, or his turn of mind. The object of Education should be to remove all obstructions and let this natural force have free play and exhibit its peculiar product. It seems to be true that no man in this is deluded. This determination of his character is to something in nature; something real. This object is called his Idea. It is that which rules his most advised actions, those especially that are most his, and is most directly discerned by him in those days and moments when he derives the sincerest satisfaction from his life.... The ancients seem to have expressed this spiritual superintendence by representing every human being as consigned to the charge of a Genius or Demon by whose counsels he was guided in what he did best.

—JOURNAL, 1834

What is your theory of education? What "Idea" rules your most advised actions?

AUGUST 2

Nature satisfies by its loveliness, and without any mixture of corporeal benefit. I see the spectacle of morning from the hilltop over against my house, from daybreak to sunrise, with emotions which an angel might share. The long slender bars of cloud float like fishes in the sea of crimson light. From the earth, as a shore, I look out into that silent sea. I seem to partake its rapid transformations: the active enchantment reaches my dust, and I dilate and conspire with the morning wind. How does Nature deify us with a few and cheap elements! Give me health and a day, and I will make the pomp of emperors ridiculous. The dawn is my Assyria; the sunset and moonrise my Paphos, and unimaginable realms of faerie; broad noon shall be my England of the senses and the understanding; the night shall be my Germany of mystic philosophy and dreams.

—NATURE

What images does nature conjure up for you? How would you describe the blessings of nature?

All that you call the world is the shadow of that substance which you are, the perpetual creation of the powers of thought, of those that are dependent and of those that are independent of your will. Do not cumber yourself with fruitless pains to mend and remedy remote effects; let the soul be erect, and all things will go well. You think me the child of my circumstances: I make my circumstance. Let any thought or motive of mine be different from that they are, the difference will transform my condition and economy. I—this thought which is called I,—is the mould into which the world is poured like melted wax. The mould is invisible, but the world betrays the shape of the mould. You call it the power of circumstance, but it is the power of me. Am I in harmony with myself? my position will seem to you just and commanding. Am I vicious and insane? my fortunes will seem to you obscure and descending. As I am, so shall I associate, and, so shall I act; Caesar's history will paint out Caesar. Jesus acted so, because he thought so. I do not wish to overlook or to gainsay any reality; I say, I make my circumstance: but if you ask me, Whence am I? I feel like other men my relation to that Fact which cannot be spoken, or defined, nor even thought, but which exists, and will exist.

— THE TRANSCENDENTALIST

Do you think that you are the child of circumstance or that we make our own circumstance? To what extent have you done so?

So use all that is called Fortune. Most men gamble with her, and gain all, and lose all, as her wheel rolls. But do thou leave as unlawful these winnings, and deal with Cause and Effect, the chancellors of God. In the Will work and acquire, and thou hast chained the wheel of Chance, and shalt sit hereafter out of fear from her rotations. A political victory, a rise of rents, the recovery of your sick, or the return of your absent friend, or some other favorable event, raises your spirits, and you think good days are preparing for you. Do not believe it. Nothing can bring you peace but yourself. Nothing can bring you peace but the triumph of principles.

—Self-Reliance

Does your peace of mind come from external events or from within? What principles to you aspire to live by?

AUGUST 5

Beware when the great God lets loose a thinker on this planet. Then all things are at risk. It is as when a conflagration has broken out in a great city, and no man knows what is safe, or where it will end. There is not a piece of science, but its flank may be turned tomorrow; there is not any literary reputation, not the so-called eternal names of fame, that may not be revised and condemned. The very hopes of man, the thoughts of his heart, the religion of nations, the manners and morals of mankind, are all at the mercy of a new generalization. Generalization is always a new influx of the divinity into the mind. Hence the thrill that attends it.

—CIRCLES

Are there thinkers on this planet now whose ideas put all things at risk? Can you name some of them?

Let a man have that profession for which God formed him that he may be useful to mankind to the whole extent of his powers, that he may find delight in the exercise of his powers, and do what he does with the full consent of his own mind. Every one knows well what difference there is in the doing things that we have with all one's heart and the doing them against one's will. If every man were engaged in those innocent things that he best loved, would not the wheels of society move with better speed and surer effect? Would not more be done and all be done better? And what an increase of happiness! For all labor would be pleasure.

—SERMON 143

Have you found your calling? Do you think most people are able to do what they feel they were meant to do?

But let us honestly state the facts. Our America has a bad name for superficialness. Great men, great nations, have not been boasters and buffoons, but perceivers of the terror of life, and have manned themselves to face it. The Spartan, embodying his religion in his country, dies before its majesty without a question. The Turk, who believes his doom is written on the iron leaf in the moment when he entered the world, rushes on the enemy's sabre with undivided will. The Turk, the Arab, the Persian, accepts the foreordained fate.... The Hindoo, under the wheel, is as firm. Our Calvinists, in the last generation, had something of the same dignity. They felt that the weight of the Universe held them down to their place. What could they do? Wise men feel that there is something which cannot be talked or voted away—a strap or belt which girds the world.... The Greek Tragedy expressed the same sense: "Whatever is fated, that will take place. The great immense mind of Jove is not to be transgressed."

—FATE

Do you consider yourself a fatalist? How do you account for that "which cannot be talked or voted away"?

AUGUST 8

Everything in the universe goes by indirection. There are no straight lines. I remember well the foreign scholar who made a week of my youth happy by his visit. "The savages in the islands," he said, "delight to play with the surf, coming in on the top of the rollers, then swimming out again, and repeat the delicious manoeuvre for hours. Well, human life is made up of such transits. There can be no greatness without abandonment. . . . Just to fill the hour,—that is happiness. Fill my hour, ye gods, so that I shall not say, whilst I have done this, 'Behold, also, an hour of my life is gone,'—but rather, 'I have lived an hour.'"

—Works and Days

Do you abandon yourself to life as the island surfers do, or do you hang back? How do you fill your hours?

AUGUST 9

Solitude is naught and society is naught. Alternate them and the good of each is seen. You can soon learn all that society can teach you for one while. A foolish routine, an indefinite multiplication of balls, concerts, rides, theatres, can teach you no more than a few can. Then retire and hide; and from the valley behold the mountain. Have solitary prayer and praise. Love the garden, the barn, the pasture, and the rock. There digest and correct the past experience, blend it with the new and divine life, and grow with God. After some interval when these delights have been sucked dry, accept again the opportunities of society. The same scenes revisited shall wear a new face, shall yield a higher culture. And so on. Undulation, Alternation, is the condition of progress, of life. Do not be an unwise churl and rail at society nor so worldly wise as to condemn solitude. But use them as conditions. Be their master, not their slave. Make circumstance,—all circumstance, conform to the law of your mind.

—JOURNAL, 1838

How are you able to balance your needs for solitude and society? How much of each do you have in your life? Is there too much of one and not enough of the other?

AUGUST 10

Each man is a new power in Nature. He holds the keys of the world in his hands. No quality in Nature's vast magazines he cannot touch, no truth he cannot see. Silent, passive, even sulkily, Nature offers every morning her wealth to man. She is immensely rich; he is welcome to her entire goods, but she speaks no word, will not so much as beckon or cough; only this, she is careful to leave all her doors ajar,—towers, hall, store-room and cellar. If he takes her hint and uses her goods she speaks no word; if he blunders and starves she says nothing. To the idle blockhead Nature is poor, sterile, inhospitable. To the gardener her loam is all strawberries, pears, pineapples. To the miller her rivers whirl the wheel and weave carpets and broad-cloth. To the sculptor her stone is soft; to the painter her plumbago and marl are pencils and chromes. To the poet all sounds and words are melodies and rhythms. In her hundred-gated Thebes every chamber is a new door.

—NATURAL HISTORY OF INTELLECT

What is the world to you? Do you make the best use of nature's gifts?

Thus to him, to this school-boy under the bending dome of day, is suggested, that he and it proceed from one root; one is leaf and one is flower; relation, sympathy, stirring in every vein. And what is that Root? Is not that the soul of his soul?—A thought too bold,—a dream too wild. Yet when this spiritual light shall have revealed the law of more earthly natures,— when he has learned to worship the soul, and to see that the natural philosophy that now is, is only the first gropings of its gigantic hand, he shall look forward to an ever expanding knowledge as to a becoming creator. He shall see, that nature is the opposite of the soul, answering to it part for part. One is seal, and one is print. Its beauty is the beauty of his own mind. Its laws are the laws of his own mind. Nature then becomes to him the measure of his attainments. So much of nature as he is ignorant of, so much of his own mind does he not yet possess. And, in fine, the ancient precept, "Know thyself," and the modern precept, "Study nature," become at last one maxim.

—THE AMERICAN SCHOLAR

Are you more aware of yourself in the presence of nature? What does nature teach you about the soul?

AUGUST 12

When the act of reflection takes place in the mind, when we look at ourselves in the light of thought, we discover that our life is embosomed in beauty. Behind us, as we go, all things assume pleasing forms, as clouds do far off. Not only things familiar and stale, but even the tragic and terrible, are comely, as they take their place in the pictures of memory. The riverbank, the weed at the water-side, the old house, the foolish person,—however neglected in the passing,—have a grace in the past. Even the corpse that has lain in the chambers has added a solemn ornament to the house. The soul will not know either deformity or pain. If, in the hours of clear reason, we should speak the severest truth, we should say, that we had never made a sacrifice. In these hours the mind seems so great, that nothing can be taken from us that seems much. All loss, all pain, is particular; the universe remains to the heart unhurt. Neither vexations nor calamities abate our trust. No man ever stated his griefs as lightly as he might. Allow for exaggeration in the most patient and sorely ridden hack that ever was driven. For it is only the finite that has wrought and suffered; the infinite lies stretched in smiling repose.

—Spiritual Laws

Does it make sense to you that the soul does not know "either deformity or pain"? Can you say that you have never made a sacrifice?

There are moods in which we court suffering, in the hope that here, at least, we shall find reality, sharp peaks and edges of truth. But it turns out to be scene-painting and counterfeit. The only thing grief has taught me, is to know how shallow it is. That, like all the rest, plays about the surface, and never introduces me into the reality, for contact with which, we would even pay the costly price of sons and lovers.... Well, souls never touch their objects. An innavigable sea washes with silent waves between us and the things we aim at and converse with. Grief too will make us idealists. In the death of my son, now more than two years ago, I seem to have lost a beautiful estate,—no more. I cannot get it nearer to me. If tomorrow I should be informed of the bankruptcy of my principal debtors, the loss of my property would be a great inconvenience to me, perhaps, for many years; but it would leave me as it found me,— neither better nor worse. So is it with this calamity: it does not touch me: some thing which I fancied was a part of me, which could not be torn away without tearing me, nor enlarged without enriching me, falls off from me, and leaves no scar. It was caducous. I grieve that grief can teach me nothing, nor carry me one step into real nature. The Indian who was laid under a curse, that the wind should not blow on him, nor water flow to him, nor fire burn him, is a type of us all. The dearest events are summer-rain, and we the Para coats that shed every drop. Nothing is left us now but death. We look to that with a grim satisfaction, saying, there at least is reality that will not dodge us.

—EXPERIENCE

Has grief ever numbed you from the experience of life? Do you ever "court suffering"?

Each man's expense must proceed from his character. As long as your genius buys, the investment is safe, though you spend like a monarch. Nature arms each man with some faculty which enables him to do easily some feat impossible to any other, and thus makes him necessary to society. This native determination guides his labor and his spending. He wants an equipment of means and tools proper to his talent. . . . Profligacy consists not in spending years of time or chests of money,—but in spending them off the line of your career. The crime which bankrupts men and states, is, job-work;—declining from your main design, to serve a turn here or there. Nothing is beneath you, if it is in the direction of your life: nothing is great or desirable, if it is off from that. I think we are entitled here to draw a straight line, and say, that society can never prosper, but must always be bankrupt, until every man does that which he was created to do.

— WEALTH

Do you spend on your genius or merely on your talent? Is your spending "in the direction of your life"?

AUGUST 15

America shall introduce pure religion. Ethics are thought not to satisfy affection. But all the religion we have is the ethics of one or another holy person. As soon as character appears, be sure love will, and veneration, and anecdotes and fables about him, and delight of good men and women in him. And, if we think what deeps of grandeur and beauty are known to us in ethical truth—the divination or insight that belongs to it...; what armor it is to protect from outward or inward harm, and with what power it converts evil accidents into benefits to good men; the power of its countenance, the power of its presence; to it alone comes true friendship,—to it, grandeur of situation and poetic perception enriching all it deals with—it will rank all other science.

—Natural Religion

For Emerson, pure religion is ethics. Do you agree? What is the essence of religion, transcending all ages and cultures?

AUGUST 16

Hitch your wagon to a star. Let us not fag in paltry works which serve our pot and bag alone. Let us not lie and steal. No god will help. We shall find all their teams going the other way,—Charles's Wain, Great Bear, Orion, Leo, Hercules: every god will leave us. Work rather for those interests which the divinities honor and promote,—justice, love, freedom, knowledge, utility.

—CIVILIZATION

What do you hitch your wagon to? Do you work "for those interests which the divinities honor and promote"?

AUGUST 17

I am sometimes discontented with my house because it lies on a dusty road and with its sills and cellar almost in the water of the meadow. But when I creep out of it into the Night or the Morning and see what majestic and what tender beauties daily wrap me in their bosom, how near to me is every transcendent secret of Nature's love and religion, I see how indifferent it is where I eat and sleep.... Then the good river-god has taken the form of my valiant Henry Thoreau here and introduced me to the riches of his shadowy starlit, moonlit stream, a lovely new world lying as close and yet as unknown to this vulgar trite one of streets and shops as death to life or poetry to prose. Through one field only we went to the boat and then left all time, all science, all history behind us and entered into Nature with one stroke of a paddle. Take care, good friend! I said, as I looked west into the sunset overhead and underneath, and he with his face toward me rowed towards it,—take care; you know not what you do, dipping your wooden oar into this en-chanted liquid, painted with all reds and purples and yellows which glows under and behind you. Presently this glory faded and the stars came and said "Here we are," and began to cast such private and ineffable beams as to stop all conversation.

—JOURNAL, 1841

Are you able to leave your cares behind when you enter into nature? Do you have a trusted companion to take walks with?

AUGUST 18

Far be from me the impatience which cannot brook the super-natural, the vast; far be from me the lust of explaining away all which appeals to the imagination, and the great presentments which haunt us. Willingly I too say, Hail! to the unknown awful powers which transcend the ken of the understanding. And the attraction which this topic has had for me and which induces me to unfold its parts before you is precisely because I think the numberless forms in which this superstition has reap-peared in every time and every people indicates the inextin-guishableness of wonder in man; betrays his conviction that behind all your explanations is a vast and potent and living Nature, inexhaustible and sublime, which you cannot explain. He is sure no book, no man has told him all. He is sure the great Instinct, the circumambient soul which flows into him as into all, and is his life, has not been searched. He is sure that intimate relations subsist between his character and his for-tunes, between him and his world; and until he can adequately tell them he will tell them widely and fabulously.

—DEMONOLOGY

What is your view of the supernatural? Is there a relationship between your character and your fortunes?

In our life and culture, everything is worked up, and comes in use,—passion, war, revolt, bankruptcy, and not less, folly and blunders, insult, ennui, and bad company. Nature is a rag-merchant, who works up every shred and ort and end into new creations; like a good chemist, whom I found, the other day, in his laboratory, converting his old shirts into pure white sugar. Life is a boundless privilege, and when you pay for your ticket, and get into the car, you have no guess what good company you shall find there. You buy much that is not rendered in the bill. Men achieve a certain greatness unawares, when working to another aim.

—Considerations By the Way

Have you ever received a gift unawares? What was it?

AUGUST 20

This over-estimate of the possibilities of Paul and Pericles, this under-estimate of our own, comes from a neglect of the fact of an identical nature.... Let a man believe in God, and not in names and places and persons. Let the great soul incarnated in some woman's form, poor and sad and single, in some Dolly or Joan, go out to service, and sweep chambers and scour floors, and its effulgent daybeams cannot be muffled or hid, but to sweep and scour will instantly appear supreme and beautiful actions, the top and radiance of human life, and all people will get mops and brooms; until, lo! suddenly the great soul has enshrined itself in some other form, and done some other deed, and that is now the flower and head of all living nature. We are the photometers, we the irritable goldleaf and tinfoil that measure the accumulations of the subtle element. We know the authentic effects of the true fire through every one of its million disguises.

— SPIRITUAL LAWS

Do you overestimate the accomplishments of people you admire and underestimate your own? Can every occupation be equally dignified?

AUGUST 21

When I converse with a profound mind, or if at any time being alone I have good thoughts, I do not at once arrive at satisfactions, as when, being thirsty, I drink water, or go to the fire, being cold: no! but I am at first apprised of my vicinity to a new and excellent region of life. By persisting to read or to think, this region gives further sign of itself, as it were in flashes of light, in sudden discoveries of its profound beauty and repose, as if the clouds that covered it parted at intervals, and showed the approaching traveller the inland mountains, with the tranquil eternal meadows spread at their base, whereon flocks graze, and shepherds pipe and dance. But every insight from this realm of thought is felt as initial, and promises a sequel. I do not make it; I arrive there, and behold what was there already. I make! O no! I clap my hands in infantine joy and amazement, before the first opening to me of this august magnificence, old with the love and homage of innumerable ages, young with the life of life, the sunbright Mecca of the desert. And what a future it opens! I feel a new heart beating with the love of the new beauty. I am ready to die out of nature, and be born again into this new yet unapproachable America I have found in the West.

—EXPERIENCE

Have you discovered "the inland mountains" of your soul? Does your reading or thinking open vistas of these inland mountains?

Let me go where e'er I will,
I hear a sky-born music still:
It sounds from all things old,
It sounds from all things young,
From all that's fair, from all that's foul,
Peals out a cheerful song.

It is not only in the rose,
It is not only in the bird,
Not only where the rainbow glows,
Nor in the song of woman heard,
But in the darkest, meanest things
There alway, alway something sings.

'Tis not in the high stars alone,
Nor in the cup of budding flowers,
Nor in the redbreast's mellow tone,
Nor in the bow that smiles in showers,
But in the mud and scum of things
There alway, alway something sings.

—Music

---

*Do you hear "skyborn music" in your life? Do you hear it
even in the difficult parts of your life?*

There are two elements that go to the composition of friendship, each so sovereign that I can detect no superiority in either, no reason why either should be first named. One is truth. A friend is a person with whom I may be sincere. Before him I may think aloud. I am arrived at last in the presence of a man so real and equal, that I may drop even those undermost garments of dissimulation, courtesy, and second thought, which men never put off, and may deal with him with the simplicity and wholeness with which one chemical atom meets another. Sincerity is the luxury allowed, like diadems and authority, only to the highest rank, that being permitted to speak truth, as having none above it to court or conform unto.... The other element of friendship is tenderness. We are holden to men by every sort of tie, by blood, by pride, by fear, by hope, by lucre, by lust, by hate, by admiration, by every circumstance and badge and trifle, but we can scarce believe that so much character can subsist in another as to draw us by love. Can another be so blessed, and we so pure, that we can offer him tenderness? When a man becomes dear to me, I have touched the goal of fortune.

—FRIENDSHIP

Do you have friends with whom you may be sincere and tender? What other qualities do you look for in a friend?

How much is lost by imitation! Our best friends may be our worst enemies. A man should learn to detect and foster that gleam of light which flashes across his mind from within far more than the luster of whole firmament without. Yet he dismisses without notice his peculiar thought *because* it is peculiar. The time will come when he will postpone all acquired knowledge to this spontaneous wisdom and will watch for this illumination more than those who watch for the morning. For this is the principle by which the other is to be arranged. This thinking would go to show the significance of self-education; that in reality there is no other; for, all the other is naught without this. *A man must teach himself* because that which each can do best, none but his maker can tell him. No man yet, knows what it is, nor can, till that person has exhibited it. Where is the master that could have taught Shakespeare? Where is the master that could have instructed Franklin or Washington or Bacon or Newton?

—JOURNAL, 1832

Have you learned to recognize "that gleam of light that flashes across your mind"? How have you educated yourself in spiritual matters?

Thy voice is sweet, Musketaquid; repeats the music of the rain; but sweeter rivers silent flit through thee, as thou through Concord plain. Thou art shut in thy banks; but the stream I love, flows in thy water, and flows through rocks and through the air, and through darkness, and through men, and women. I hear and see the inundation and eternal spending of the stream, in winter and in summer, in men and animals, in passion and thought. Happy are they who can hear it. I see thy brimming, eddying stream, and thy enchantment. For thou change every rock in thy bed into a gem: all is real opal and agate, and at will thou pavest with diamonds. Take them away from thy stream, and they are poor shards and flints: so it is with me today.

—JOURNAL, 1856

Do you feel the stream of life flowing through you? Do you ever feel alienated from the stream of life?

We must be lovers, and at once the impossible becomes possible. Our age and history, for these thousand years, has not been the history of kindness, but of selfishness. Our distrust is very expensive. The money we spend for courts and prisons is very ill laid out. We make, by distrust, the thief, and burglar, and incendiary, and by our court and jail we keep him so. An acceptance of the sentiment of love throughout Christendom for a season, would bring the felon and the outcast to our side in tears, with the devotion of his faculties to our service. See this wide society of laboring men and women. We allow ourselves to be served by them, we live apart from them, and meet them without a salute in the streets. We do not greet their talents, nor rejoice in their good fortune, nor foster their hopes, nor in the assembly of the people vote for what is dear to them. Thus we enact the part of the selfish noble and king from the foundation of the world.

—Man the Reformer

How would society be different if it were based on love instead of distrust? Do you love or distrust your fellow human beings? Do you greet those who serve you? Do you know their names?

I do not wish to expiate, but to live. My life is for itself and not for a spectacle. I much prefer that it should be of a lower strain, so it be genuine and equal, than that it should be glittering and unsteady.... What I must do is all that concerns me, not what the people think. This rule, equally arduous in actual and in intellectual life, may serve for the whole distinction between greatness and meanness. It is the harder, because you will always find those who think they know what is your duty better than you know it. It is easy in the world to live after the world's opinion; it is easy in solitude to live after our own; but the great man is he who in the midst of the crowd keeps with perfect sweetness the independence of solitude.

—SELF-RELIANCE

Do you aspire to do what concerns you rather than what people think you should do? Is this a selfish and egocentric way to live?

Revelation is the disclosure of the soul. The popular notion of revelation is, that it is a telling of fortunes. In past oracles of the soul the understanding seeks to find answers to sensual questions, and undertakes to tell from God how long men shall exist, what their hands shall do, and who shall be their company, adding names, and dates, and places. But we must pick no locks. We must check this low curiosity. An answer in words is delusive; it is really no answer to the questions you ask. Do not require a description of the countries towards which you sail. The description does not describe them to you, and tomorrow you arrive there, and know them by inhabiting them. Men ask concerning the immortality of the soul, the employments of heaven, the state of the sinner, and so forth.... Never a moment did that sublime spirit speak in their *patois*."

—THE OVER-SOUL

How would you describe revelation? Is it like the telling of fortunes?

Motion or change, and identity or rest, are the first and second secrets of nature: Motion and Rest. The whole code of her laws may be written on the thumbnail, or the signet of a ring. The whirling bubble on the surface of a brook, admits us to the secret of the mechanics of the sky. Every shell on the beach is a key to it. A little water made to rotate in a cup explains the formation of the simpler shells; the addition of matter from year to year, arrives at last at the most complex forms; and yet so poor is nature with all her craft, that, from the beginning to the end of the universe, she has but one stuff,—but one stuff with its two ends, to serve up all her dream-like variety. Compound it how she will, star, sand, fire, water, tree, man, it is still one stuff, and betrays the same properties.

—Nature

Do you feel of "one stuff" with the rest of nature? How do motion and rest affect your life?

Spiritual religion has no other evidence than its own intrinsic probability. It is probable because the mind is so constituted as that they [its laws] appear likely so to be. It never scolds. It simply describes the laws of moral nature as the naturalist does physical [laws] and shows the surprising beauties and terrors of human life. It never scolds and never sneers. It is opposed to Calvinism in this respect that all spiritual truths are self-evident, but the doctrines of Calvin are not, and are not pretended to be by their understanding defenders of mystery. This is the only live religion. All others are dead or formal. This cannot be but in the new conviction of the mind. Others may. This produces instant and infinite abuses. It is a two-edged sword because it condemns forms but supplies a better law only to the living. It leaves the dead to bury their dead. The popular religion is an excellent constable, the true religion is God himself to the believer and maketh him a perfect lover of the whole world; but it is only a cloak of licentiousness to the rest. It would dismiss all bad preachers and do great harm to society by taking off restraints.

—JOURNAL, 1834

What is the difference between spirituality and religion? Are human beings innately religious? What arguments against spirituality do you hear today?

A moral sentiment rules all our intercourse; when we glance into each other's eyes, when we meet, when we part, we accuse or excuse each other. The structure of animals in whole or in each part, seems to derive from a moral sentiment, from beneficent will. The world is all welded, and kneaded, and cast into mould by moral force. These are the powers amidst we live, these are the angles that take us by the hand, these immortal, invulnerable guardians. By their strength we are strong, and, on signal occasions in our career, their inspirations flow to us, and make the simple, wise; the weak, able; and the timid, brave; make the selfish, and protected, and tenderly bred person strong for his duty, make the boy able to serve his country, ready to sacrifice, ready to be sacrificed, wise in counsel, skilful in action, competent to rule, willing to obey, equal to the occasions of this passing world, and calmly waiting the revelations of the future.

—MORAL FORCES

Do we live in a moral universe, subject to moral forces?
Where do you think morality comes from?

SEPTEMBER

Meditations

SEPTEMBER 1

I will not live out of me
I will not see with other's eyes
My good is good, my evil ill
I would be free—I cannot be
While I take things as others please to rate them
I dare attempt to lay out my own road
That which myself delights in shall be Good
That which I do not want,—indifferent,
That which I hate is Bad. That's flat
Henceforth, please God, forever I forego
The yoke of men's opinions. I will be
Lighthearted as a bird and live with God.
I find him in the bottom of my heart
I hear continually his Voice therein...
Who says the heart's a blind guide? It is not.
My heart never did counsel me to sin
I wonder where it got its wisdom
For in the darkest maze amid the sweetest baits
Or amid horrid dangers never once
Did that gentle Angel fail of his oracle
The little needle always knows the north...
And this wise Seer never errs
I never taught it what it teaches me
I only follow when I act aright.

—Self-Reliance

Do you rely on your own inner compass to know what's right and wrong? Have you ever felt that your best self was compromised by the expectations of others?

The ground of hope is in the infinity of the world; which infinity reappears in every particle, the powers of all society in every individual, and of all mind in every mind. I know against all appearances that the universe can receive no detriment; that there is a remedy for every wrong and a satisfaction for every soul. Here is this wonderful thought. But whence came it? Who put it in the mind? It was not I, it was not you; it is elemental,—belongs to thought and virtue, and whenever we have either we see the beams of this light. When the Master of the universe has points to carry in his government he impresses his will in the structure of minds.

—IMMORTALITY

Do you find hope in the infinity of the world? Do you think that natural laws are impressed in "the structure of minds"?

The intellectual life may be kept clean and healthful, if man will live the life of nature, and not import into his mind difficulties which are none of his. No man need be perplexed in his speculations. Let him do and say what strictly belongs to him, and, though very ignorant of books, his nature shall not yield him any intellectual obstructions and doubts. Our young people are diseased with the theological problems of original sin, origin of evil, predestination, and the like. These never presented a practical difficulty to any man,—never darkened across any man's road, who did not go out of his way to seek them. These are the soul's mumps, and measles, and whooping-coughs, and those who have not caught them cannot describe their health or prescribe the cure. A simple mind will not know these enemies.

—SPIRITUAL LAWS

Do you agree with Emerson's view of sin and evil? Have you tried to cultivate a simple mind?

SEPTEMBER 4

But Nature is no sentimentalist,—does not cosset or pamper us. We must see that the world is rough and surly, and will not mind drowning a man or a woman; but swallows your ship like a grain of dust. The cold, inconsiderate of persons, tingles your blood, benumbs your feet, freezes a man like an apple. The diseases, the elements, fortune, gravity, lightning, respect no persons. The way of Providence is a little rude. The habit of snake and spider, the snap of the tiger and other leapers and bloody jumpers, the crackle of the bones of his prey in the coil of the anaconda,—these are in the system, and our habits are like theirs.... The planet is liable to shocks from comets, perturbations from planets, rendings from earthquake and volcano, alterations of climate, precessions of equinoxes. Rivers dry up by opening of the forest. The sea changes its bed. Towns and counties fall into it. At Lisbon, an earthquake killed men like flies. At Naples, three years ago, ten thousand persons were crushed in a few minutes.

—Fate

What is your view of nature? How do you account for natural evil?

Democracy, Freedom has its root in the sacred truth that every man hath in him the divine Reason, or that though few men since the creation of the world live according to the dictates of Reason, yet all men are created capable of so doing. That is the equality and the only equality of all men. To this truth we look when we say, "Reverence thyself. Be true to thyself." Because every man has within him somewhat really divine, therefore is slavery the unpardonable outrage it is.

—JOURNAL, 1834

What do you think all human beings hold in common? What would happen if all people reverenced themselves? Would this be a good or a bad thing?

SEPTEMBER 6

Let our affection flow out to our fellows; it would operate in a day the greatest of all revolutions. It is better to work on institutions by the sun than by the wind. The state must consider the poor man, and all voices must speak for him. Every child that is born must have a just chance for his bread. Let the amelioration in our laws of property proceed from the concession of the rich, not from the grasping of the poor. Let us begin by habitual imparting. Let us understand that the equitable rule is, that no one should take more than his share, let him be ever so rich. Let me feel that I am to be a lover. I am to see to it that the world is the better for me, and to find my reward in the act. Love would put a new face on this weary old world in which we dwell as pagans and enemies too long, and it would warm the heart to see how fast the vain diplomacy of statesmen, the impotence of armies, and navies, and lines of defence, would be superceded by this unarmed child.... This great, overgrown, dead Christendom of ours still keeps alive at least the name of a lover of mankind. But one day all men will be lovers; and every calamity will be dissolved in the universal sunshine.

—MAN THE REFORMER

What would it take to establish the law of love in human relations? Do you consider yourself a lover?

I do not wish to treat friendships daintily, but with roughest courage. When they are real, they are not glass threads or frost-work, but the solidest thing we know. For now, after so many ages of experience, what do we know of nature, or of ourselves? Not one step has man taken toward the solution of the problem of his destiny. In one condemnation of folly stand the whole universe of men. But the sweet sincerity of joy and peace, which I draw from this alliance with my brother's soul, is the nut itself, whereof all nature and all thought is but the husk and shell. Happy is the house that shelters a friend! It might well be built, like a festal bower or arch, to entertain him a single day. Happier, if he know the solemnity of that relation, and honor its law!

—FRIENDSHIP

Are your friendships "the solidest thing" you know? Do you "know the solemnity of that relation and honor its law"?

Spend after your genius, and by system. Nature goes by rule, not by sallies and salutations. There must be system in the economies. Saving and unexpensiveness will not keep the most pathetic family from ruin, nor will bigger incomes make free spending safe. The secret of success lies never in the amount of money, but in the relation of income to outgo; as if, after expense has been fixed at a certain point, then new and steady rills of income, though never so small, being added, wealth begins. But in ordinary, as means increase, spending increases faster, so that, large incomes, in England and elsewhere, are found not to help matters.... In England, the richest country in the universe, I was assured by shrewd observers, that great lords and ladies had no more guineas to give away than other people; that liberality with money is as rare, and as immediately famous a virtue as it is here. Want is a growing giant whom the coat of Have was never large enough to cover.

— WEALTH

Do you find that want is a growing giant in your life? Are you able to distinguish between desires and needs?

Providence supports but does not spoil its children. We are called sons, not darlings, of the Deity. There is ever good in store for those who love it; knowledge for those who seek it; and if we do evil, we suffer the consequences of evil. Throughout the administration of the world there is the same aspect of stern kindness; of good against your will; good against your good; ten thousand channels of active beneficence, but all flowing with the same regard to general, not particular, profit.... And to such an extent is this great statute policy of God carried, that many, nay, most, of the great blessings of humanity require cycles of a thousand years to bring them to their height.

—JOURNAL, 1824

Do you believe in providence? Is the universe tending toward the good, or is it a random and meaningless affair?

Who looks upon a river in a meditative hour, and is not reminded of the flux of all things? Throw a stone into the stream, and the circles that propagate themselves are the beautiful type of all influence. Man is conscious of a universal soul within or behind his individual life, wherein, as in a firmament, the natures of Justice, Truth, Love, Freedom, arise and shine. This universal soul, he calls Reason: it is not mine, or thine, or his, but we are its; we are its property and men. And the blue sky in which the private earth is buried, the sky with its eternal calm, and full of everlasting orbs, is the type of Reason. That which, intellectually considered, we call Reason, considered in relation to nature, we call Spirit. Spirit is the Creator. Spirit hath life in itself. And man in all ages and countries, embodies it in his language, as *Father*.

—NATURE

Are you conscious of "a universal soul within or behind our individual life"? How are you related to it?

SEPTEMBER 11

A foolish consistency is the hobgoblin of little minds, adored by little statesmen and philosophers and divines. With consistency a great soul has simply nothing to do. He may as well concern himself with his shadow on the wall. Speak what you think now in hard words, and tomorrow speak what tomorrow thinks in hard words again, though it contradict every thing you said today.—"Ah, so you shall be sure to be misunderstood."—Is it so bad, then, to be misunderstood? Pythagoras was misunderstood, and Socrates, and Jesus, and Luther, and Copernicus, and Galileo, and Newton, and every pure and wise spirit that ever took flesh. To be great is to be misunderstood.

—SELF-RELIANCE

Do you aspire to be consistent? Are you satisfied to be inconsistent and misunderstood?

SEPTEMBER 12

If I have described life as a flux of moods, I must now add, that there is that in us which changes not, and which ranks all sensations and states of mind. The consciousness in each man is a sliding scale, which identifies him now with the First Cause, and now with the flesh of his body; life above life, in infinite degrees. The sentiment from which it sprung determines the dignity of any deed, and the question ever is, not, what you have done or forborne, but, at whose command you have done or forborne it.

—EXPERIENCE

Is there something within you that does not change with age and the flux of moods and fortunes? Is it a source of guidance for you?

Each nation prefers its own Bible: the Chinese, his Mencius and Confucius, the Hindoo, his *Vedas*, the Persian, his *Desatir*, the Buddhist, his *Mahawanso*, the Arab, his *Koran*, like villagers who each magnify his own meetinghouse and town hall. But one day they meet and become acquainted, and find that each expresses the same sense which is dear to all.... These, and such as these, are the teachings of the conscience and the strivings of the intellect, and yet this eager reference to the future is not quite philosophical. That which befits us embosomed in beauty and wonder as we are is cheerfulness, and activity, and the endeavor to realize our aspirations.

—NATURAL RELIGION

Do you believe in the universality of all religions? What would you say is their core teaching?

SEPTEMBER 14

In stripping time of its illusions, in seeking to find what is the heart of the day, we come to the quality of the moment, and drop the duration altogether. It is the depth at which we live and not at all the surface extension that imports. We pierce to the eternity, of which time is the flitting surface; and, really, the least acceleration of thought and the least increase of power of thought, make life to seem and to be of vast duration. We call it time; but when that acceleration and that deepening take effect, it acquires another and a higher name.

—Works and Days

Is it the depth rather than the length of life that is most important? Have you ever experienced a "pierce to the eternity"?

SEPTEMBER 15

In reckoning the sources of our mental power it were fatal to omit that one which pours all the others into its mould;—that unknown country in which all the rivers of our knowledge have their fountains, and which, by its qualities and structure, determines both the nature of the waters and the direction in which they flow. The healthy mind lies in parallel to the currents of Nature and sees things in place, or makes discoveries. Newton did not exercise more ingenuity but less than another to see the world. Right thought comes spontaneously, comes like the morning wind; comes daily, like our daily bread, to humble service; comes duly to those who look for it. It does not need to pump your brains and force thought to think rightly. Oh no, the ingenious person is warped by his ingenuity and mis-sees.

—NATURAL HISTORY OF INTELLECT

Have you ever wished to explore "that unknown country in which the rivers of our knowledge have their fountains"? How have you tried to align your thinking with "the currents of Nature"?

SEPTEMBER 16

There is one mind common to all individual men. Every man is an inlet to the same and to all of the same. He that is once admitted to the right of reason is made a freeman of the whole estate. What Plato has thought, he may think; what a saint has felt, he may feel; what at any time has befallen any man, he can understand. Who hath access to this universal mind is a party to all that is or can be done, for this is the only and sovereign agent.

—HISTORY

Do you believe in a "universal mind"? How might we have access to it?

SEPTEMBER 17

In the high sense of instinct it may be called our primary Teacher in so great a latitude as almost to exclude all other teaching. For that sentiment of essential life, the sense of being which in calm hours rises, we know not how, in the soul, is not diverse from things,—from the sky, from light, from time, from man, but one with them and proceedeth obviously from the same source whence their life and being also proceedeth and so we owe it an infinite reverence, for in our condition, and in the natures of men and things around us, we see only the secondary or modified effects of the one Soul. All men are taught of this and hence our uniform belief in the unlimited possibilities of every man. For when I see the doors by which God entereth into the mind and that there is no sot nor fop nor ruffian, nor pedant, into whom thoughts do not enter by passages which the individual never left open, I can expect any revolution in character. The co-presence of the living soul is essential to all teaching. The informations of the soul are so great in amount that, (where they are received and obeyed,) they degrade all other teachings into mere organs and apparatus.

— THE SCHOOL

Do you consider instinct or intuition to be your primary teacher? Do you feel you can trust your instincts?

SEPTEMBER 18

An immoral law makes it a man's duty to break it, at every hazard. For Virtue is the very self of every man. It is therefore a principle of law, that an immoral contract is void, and that an immoral statute is void. For, as laws do not make right, but are simply declaratory of a right which already existed, it is not to be presumed that they can so stultify themselves as to command injustice.

It is remarkable how rare in the history of tyrants is an immoral law. Some color, some indirection was always used. If you take up the volumes of the "Universal History," you will find it difficult searching. The precedents are few. It is not easy to parallel the wickedness of this American law. And that is the head and body of this discontent, that the law is immoral. Here is a statute which enacts the crime of kidnapping,—a crime on one footing with arson and murder. A man's right to liberty is as inalienable as his right to life.

—On the Fugitive Slave Law

Do you believe it is your right and duty to break immoral laws? How do you know whether a law is immoral or simply one you do not agree with?

SEPTEMBER 19

In the woods, this afternoon, it seemed plain to me, that most men were Pantheists at heart, say what they might of their theism. No other path is, indeed, open for them to the One, intellectually at least. Man delights in freedom even to license, and claims infinite indulgence, from the Powers seen, and unseen, to whom he would give indulgence on those terms. In a word, he would conquer and surrender in his own way; living no less open to the power of the soul than of the State, swayed by gods and demons, he is never, in his fresh morning-love, quite himself. His audacity is immense. His impieties are his pieties: he wins and loses, to win and lose. He reveres, dallies with, defies, and overcomes every god and demigod of the Pantheon, in quest of his freedom, and thus liberates Humanity from the demons by these twelve labors.

—JOURNAL, 1856

Emerson suggests that most people are pantheists at heart. Would you agree? Do you consider yourself a pantheist?

It is inevitable to name particulars of virtue and of condition, and to exaggerate them. But all rests at last on that integrity which dwarfs talent and can spare it. Sanity consists in not being subdued by your means. Fancy prices are paid for position and for the culture of talent, but to the grand interests, superficial success if of no account.... The secret of culture is to learn, that a few great points steadily reappear, alike in the poverty of the obscurest farm, and in the miscellany of metropolitan life, and that these few are alone to be regarded—the escape from all false ties; courage to be what we are; and love of what is simple and beautiful; independence, and cheerful relation, these are the essentials— these, and the wish to serve— to add somewhat to the well-being of men.

—CONSIDERATIONS BY THE WAY

Do "a few great points steadily reappear" for you? How would you describe them?

SEPTEMBER 21

Dream delivers us to dream, and there is no end to illusion. Life is a train of moods like a string of beads, and, as we pass through them, they prove to be many-colored lenses which paint the world their own hue, and each shows only what lies in its focus. From the mountain you see the mountain. We animate what we can, and we see only what we animate.... There are always sunsets, and there is always genius; but only a few hours so serene that we can relish nature or criticism. The more or less depends on structure or temperament. Temperament is the iron wire on which the beads are strung.... Of what use to make heroic vows of amendment, if the same old law-breaker is to keep them? What cheer can the religious sentiment yield, when that is suspected to be secretly dependent on the seasons of the year, and the state of the blood?... We see young men who owe us a new world, so readily and lavishly they promise, but they never acquit the debt; they die young and dodge the account: or if they live, they lose themselves in the crowd.

—EXPERIENCE

How would you describe your temperament? Is one's spiritual life regulated by one's temperament?

It is essential that he [the genuine man] should believe in himself because that is the object in view, to raise up a great counterbalance to the engrossing of riches, of popularity, of the love of life in the man and make him feel that all these ought to be his servants and not his masters, that he is as great, nay much greater, than any of these: to make him feel that whereas the consequences of most men now depends on their wealth or their popularity, he is capable of being sought to become a man so rich and so commanding by the simple force of his character, that wealth or poverty would be an unnoticed accident, that his solitary opinion and his support to any cause whatever would be like the acclamation of the world in its behalf. This as we shall see is the secret of all true greatness, the development of the inward nature, the raising to its true place, to absolute sovereignty, harkening to this voice which to most men sounds so faint and insignificant above the thunder of the laws and the customs of mankind. And it is founded and can only be founded in religion. It can only prefer this self because it esteems it to speak the voice of God.

—SERMON 164

What place do integrity and authenticity hold in your values? Have you ever felt that you entertained "a solitary opinion"? What did you do with it?

It seems to me as if the high idea of Culture as the end of existence, does not pervade the mind of the thinking people of our community; the conviction that a discovering of human power to which the trades and occupations they follow, the connexions they form, and the motley tissue of their common experience are quite subordinate and auxiliary: is the main interest of history. Could this be properly taught, I think it must provoke and overmaster the young and ambitious, and yield rich fruits. Culture in the high sense does not consist in polishing or varnishing but in so presenting the attractions of Nature that the slumbering attributes of man may burst their iron sleep and rush full-grown into day. Culture is not the trimming and turfing of gardens, but the showing the true harmony of the unshorn landscape with horrid thickets and bald mountains and the balance of the land and sea.

—JOURNAL, 1837

Does Emerson's notion of culture exist to any degree today? Have you experienced the discovery of human power in the pursuit of culture?

SEPTEMBER 24

Talk with a seaman of the hazards to life in his profession, and he will ask you, "Where are the old sailors? Do you not see that all are young men?" And we, on this sea of human thought, in like manner inquire, Where are the old idealists? where are they who represented to the last generation that extravagant hope, which a few happy aspirants suggest to ours?... Are they dead—taken in early ripeness to the gods,—as ancient wisdom foretold their fate? Or did the high idea die out of them, and leave their unperfumed body as its tomb and tablet, announcing to all that the celestial inhabitant, who once gave them beauty, had departed? Will it be better with the new generation?

—THE TRANSCENDENTALIST

Emerson suggests that idealism abates with age. Do you agree? Were you an idealist in your youth? Are you still?

SEPTEMBER 25

These questions which we lust to ask about the future are a confession of sin. God has no answer for them. No answer in words can reply to a question of things. It is not in an arbitrary "decree of God," but in the nature of man, that a veil shuts down on the facts of tomorrow; for the soul will not have us read any other cipher than that of cause and effect. By this veil, which curtains events, it instructs the children of men to live in today. The only mode of obtaining an answer to these questions of the senses is to forego all low curiosity, and, accepting the tide of being which floats us into the secret of nature, work and live, work and live, and all unawares the advancing soul has built and forged for itself a new condition, and the question and the answer are one.

— THE OVER-SOUL

Are you able to live in today? Do you think your soul is advancing?

You cannot hide any secret. If the artist succor his flagging spirits by opium or wine, his work will characterize itself as the effect of opium or wine. If you make a picture or a statue, it sets the beholder in that state of mind you had, when you made it. If you spend for show, on building, or gardening, or on pictures, or on equipages, it will so appear. We are all physiognomists and penetrators of character, and things themselves are detective. If you follow the suburban fashion in building a sumptuous-looking house for a little money, it will appear to all eyes as a cheap dear house. There is no privacy that cannot be penetrated. No secret can be kept in the civilized world. Society is a masked ball, where every one hides his real character, and reveals it by hiding. If a man wish to conceal anything he carries, those whom he meets know that he conceals somewhat, and usually know what he conceals.

— Worship

Do you spend for show? Do you agree that "no secret can be kept in the civilized world"?

SEPTEMBER 27

And what else is life? We hoe all day or curry horses or sell stocks or read books and a moment of serenity and sight intercalates the routine one patch of blue sky which presently is lost again amid all these fogs. In the progress of character the Blue will vein and reticulate the whole web of particulars. But now we live sentences like these Asiatic sages.

—JOURNAL, 1841

What do you do all day? Do you occasionally catch a glimpse of blue sky?

Each age, it is found, must write its own books; or rather, each generation for the next succeeding.... Yet hence arises a grave mischief. The sacredness which attaches to the act of creation—the act of thought,—is transferred to the record. The poet chanting, was felt to be a divine man: henceforth the chant is divine also. The writer was a just and wise spirit: henceforward it is settled, the book is perfect; as love of the hero corrupts into worship of his statue. Instantly, the book becomes noxious: the guide is a tyrant. The sluggish and perverted mind of the multitude, slow to open to the incursions of Reason, having once so opened, having once received this book, stands upon it, and makes an outcry, if it is disparaged. Colleges are built on it. Books are written on it by thinkers, not by Man Thinking; by men of talent, that is, who start wrong, who set out from accepted dogmas, not from their own sight of principles. Meek young men grow up in libraries, believing it their duty to accept the views, which Cicero, which Locke, which Bacon, have given, forgetful that Cicero, Locke, and Bacon were only young men in libraries, when they wrote these books.... Hence, instead of Man Thinking, we have the bookworm.

— THE AMERICAN SCHOLAR

Do you share Emerson's view of books? Can reading be creative?

The soul's advances are not made by gradation, such as can be represented by motion in a straight line; but rather by ascension of state, such as can be represented by metamorphosis,—from the egg to the worm, from the worm to the fly. The growths of genius are of a certain *total* character, that does not advance the elect individual first over John, then Adam, then Richard, and give to each the pain of discovered inferiority, but by every throe of growth the man expands there where he works, passing, at each pulsation, classes, populations, of men. With each divine impulse the mind rends the thin rinds of the visible and finite, and comes out into eternity, and inspires and expires its air. It converses with truths that have always been spoken in the world, and becomes conscious of a closer sympathy with Zeno and Arrian, than with persons in the house.

—THE OVER-SOUL

Have you felt that your spiritual growth has been a kind of metamorphosis? Are you able to understand truths that you didn't understand before?

While the immense energy of the sentiment of duty and the awe of the supernatural exert incomparable influence on the mind,—yet it is often perverted, and the tradition received with awe, but without correspondent action of the receiver. Then you find so many men infatuated on that topic! Wise on all other, they lose their head the moment they talk of religion. It is the sturdiest prejudice in the public mind that religion is something by itself; a department distinct from all other experiences, and to which the tests and judgment men are ready enough to show on other things, do not apply. You may sometimes talk with the gravest and best citizen, and the moment the topic of religion is broached, he runs into a childish superstition. His face looks infatuated, and his conversation is. When I talked with an ardent missionary, and pointed out to him that his creed found no support in my experience, he replied, "It is not so in your experience, but is so in the other world." I answer: Other world! There is no other world. God is one and omnipresent; here or nowhere is the whole fact. The one miracle which God works evermore is in Nature, and imparting himself to the mind. When we ask simply, "What is true in thought? what is just in action?" it is the yielding of the private heart to the Divine mind, and all personal preferences, and all requiring of wonders, are profane.

—THE SOVEREIGNTY OF ETHICS

Is religion is "a department distinct from all other experiences"? Do you believe in another world, or do you agree with Emerson that "God is one and omnipresent, here or nowhere"?

OCTOBER

Meditations

OCTOBER 1

A man contains all that is needful to his government within himself. He is made a law unto himself. All real good or evil that can befall him must be from himself. He can only do himself any good or any harm. Nothing can be given to him or taken from him but there is always a compensation. There is a correspondence between the human soul and everything that exists in the world,—more properly, everything that is known to man. Instead of studying things without the principles of them, all may be penetrated unto within him. Every act puts the agent in a new condition. The purpose of life seems to be to acquaint a man with himself. He is not to live to the future as described to him but to live to the real future by living to the real present. The highest revelation is that God is in every man.

—JOURNAL, 1833

Do you believe, as Emerson does, that "the highest revelation" is that God is in every person? Would you agree that the purpose of life is "to acquaint us with ourselves"?

OCTOBER 2

Our doctrine must begin with the necessary and eternal, and discriminate Fate from the necessary; there is no limitation about the Eternal. Thought, Will, is co-eternal with the world; and, as soon as intellect is awaked in any man, it shares so far of the eternity,—is of the maker, not of the made. But Fate is the name we give to the action of that one eternal, all-various necessity on the brute myriads, whether in things, animals, or in men in whom the intellect pore is not yet opened. To such it is only a burning wall which hurts those who run against it. The great day in the man is the birth of perception, which instantly throws him on the party of the Eternal. He sees what must be, and that it is not more that which must be, than it is that which should be, or what is best. To be then becomes the infinite good, and breath is jubilation. A breath of Will blows through the universe eternally in the direction of the right or necessary; it is the air which all intellects inhale and exhale, and all things are blown or moved by it in order and orbit.

—JOURNAL, 1859

Do you believe in fate? Do you think fate and will can be reconciled?

OCTOBER 3

A new disease has fallen on the life of man. Every Age, like every human body, has its own distemper. Other times have had war, or famine, or a barbarism domestic or bordering, as their antagonism. Our forefathers walked in the world and went to their graves, tormented with the fear of Sin, and the terror of the Day of Judgment. These terrors have lost their force, and our torment is Unbelief, the Uncertainty as to what we ought to do; the distrust of the value of what we do, and the distrust that the Necessity (which we all at last believe in) is fair and beneficent. Our Religion assumes the negative form of rejection. Out of love of the true, we repudiate the false: and the Religion is an abolishing criticism. A great perplexity hangs like a cloud on the brow of all cultivated persons, a certain imbecility in the best spirits, which distinguishes the period.... We mistrust every step we take. We find it the worst thing about time, that we know not what to do with it.

—INTRODUCTORY LECTURE ON THE TIMES

Do you agree with Emerson that skepticism or unbelief is the peculiar disease of our time? Are you uncertain about the future and what we ought to do?

The inquiry leads us to that source, at once the essence of genius, of virtue, and of life, which we call Spontaneity or Instinct. We denote this primary wisdom as Intuition, whilst all later teachings are tuitions. In that deep force, the last fact behind which analysis cannot go, all things find their common origin. For, the sense of being which in calm hours rises, we know not how, in the soul, is not diverse from things, from space, from light, from time, from man, but one with them, and proceeds obviously from the same source whence their life and being also proceed. We first share the life by which things exist, and afterwards see them as appearances in nature, and forget that we have shared their cause. Here is the fountain of action and of thought. Here are the lungs of that inspiration which giveth man wisdom, and which cannot be denied without impiety and atheism. We lie in the lap of immense intelligence, which makes us receivers of its truth and organs of its activity. When we discern justice, when we discern truth, we do nothing of ourselves, but allow a passage to its beams. If we ask whence this comes, if we seek to pry into the soul that causes, all philosophy is at fault. Its presence or its absence is all we can affirm. Every man discriminates between the voluntary acts of his mind, and his involuntary perceptions, and knows that to his involuntary perceptions a perfect faith is due. He may err in the expression of them, but he knows that these things are so, like day and night, not to be disputed.

—SELF-RELIANCE

What credence do you give to your instincts and intuitions?
Do you have "a perfect faith" in your involuntary perceptions?

OCTOBER 5

The great distinction between teachers sacred or literary,...
between men of the world, who are reckoned accomplished
talkers, and here and there a fervent mystic, prophesying half
insane under the infinitude of his thought,—is, that one class
speak *from within*, or from experience, as parties and possessors
of the fact; and the other class, *from without*, as spectators
merely, or perhaps as acquainted with the fact on the evidence
of third persons. It is of no use to preach to me from without. I
can do that too easily myself. Jesus speaks always from within,
and in a degree that transcends all others. In that is the miracle. I believe beforehand that it ought so to be. All men stand
continually in the expectation of the appearance of such a
teacher. But if a man do not speak from within the veil, where
the word is one with that it tells of, let him lowly confess it.

—THE OVER-SOUL

---

*Have you had teachers whom you felt spoke "from within, or
from experience"? What religious figures do you think have
spoken from within?*

OCTOBER 6

There are days which occur in this climate, at almost any season of the year, wherein the world reaches its perfection, when the air, the heavenly bodies, and the earth, make a harmony, as if nature would indulge her offspring; when, in these bleak upper sides of the planet, nothing is to desire that we have heard of the happiest latitudes, and we bask in the shining hours of Florida and Cuba; when everything that has life gives sign of satisfaction. . . . These halcyons may be looked for with a little more assurance in that pure October weather, which we distinguish by the name of the Indian Summer. The day, immeasurably long, sleeps over the broad hills and warm wide fields. To have lived through all its sunny hours, seems longevity enough. The solitary places do not seem quite lonely. At the gates of the forest, the surprised man of the world is forced to leave his city estimates of great and small, wise and foolish. The knapsack of custom falls off his back with the first step he makes into these precincts. Here is sanctity which shames our religions, and reality which discredits our heroes. Here we find nature to be the circumstance which dwarfs every other circumstance, and judges like a god all men that come to her.

— NATURE

Have you had days that seemed perfect to you? Do you find a sanity in nature that "shames our religions"?

OCTOBER 7

Be genuine. Be girt with truth. Aim in all things, at all times to be that within which you would appear without. Commune with your own heart that you may learn what it means to be true to yourself and follow that guidance steadily. God would have you introduce another standard of success than that which prevails in the world. When you go home at night, and cast your thoughts on your condition, fix them upon your character: instead of asking if this day has made you richer, or better known, or what compliments you have received, you shall ask—am I more just—am I more useful—more patient—more wise—what have I learned—what new truth has been disclosed to me? Then you will have an interest in yourself. You will be watching the wonderful opening and growth of a human character, the birth and growth of an angel that has been born, but never will die—who was designed by his maker to be a benefactor to the world, and to find his own happiness in forever enlarging the knowledge, multiplying the powers, and exalting the pleasures of others.

—SERMON 164

When you go home at night, what do you your thoughts dwell on? Has any new truth been revealed to you?

OCTOBER 8

We stand on the edge of all that is great yet are restrained in inactivity and unconscious of our powers.... We are always on the brink of an ocean of thought into which we do not yet swim.... There is much preparation... often with little fruit. But suddenly in any place, in the street, in the chamber, will the heaven open, and the regions of wisdom be uncovered, as if to show how thin the veil, how null the circumstances. As quickly, a Lethean stream washes through us and bereaves us of ourselves.... What a benefit if a rule could be given whereby the mind dreaming amidst the gross fogs of matter, could at any moment east itself and find the Sun. But the common life is an endless succession of phantasms. And long after we have deemed ourselves recovered and sound, light breaks in upon us and we find that we have yet had no sane hour. Another morn rises on mid-noon.

—JOURNAL, 1835

Have you ever found yourself "dreaming amid the gross fogs of matter"? How did you restore yourself?

OCTOBER 9

All things are moral; and in their boundless changes have an unceasing reference to spiritual nature. Therefore is nature glorious with form, color, and motion, that every globe in the remotest heaven; every chemical change from the rudest crystal up to the laws of life; every change of vegetation from the first principle of growth in the eye of a leaf, to the tropical forest and antediluvian coal-mine; every animal function from the sponge up to Hercules, shall hint or thunder to man the laws of right and wrong, and echo the Ten Commandments. Therefore is Nature ever the ally of Religion: lends all her pomp and riches to the religious sentiment. . . . The moral law lies at the center of nature and radiates to the circumference. It is the pith and marrow of every substance, every relation, and every process. All things with which we deal, preach to us. What is a farm but a mute gospel? . . . Nor can it be doubted that this moral sentiment which thus scents the air, grows in the grain, and impregnates the waters of the world, is caught by man and sinks into his soul. Herein is especially apprehended the unity of Nature,—the unity in variety,—which meets us everywhere. All the endless variety of things make an identical impression. . . . A leaf, a drop, a crystal, a moment of time is related to the whole, and partakes of the perfection of the whole. Each particle is a microcosm, and faithfully renders the likeness of the world.

—NATURE

Do you believe, as Emerson does, that there are moral laws as well as physical ones? Are nature and our experience of nature the basis of our religion and morality?

OCTOBER 10

It is not to be denied that there must be some wide difference between my faith and other faith; and mine is a certain brief experience, which surprised me in the highway or in the market, in some place, at some time,—whether in the body or out of the body, God knoweth,—and made me aware that I had played the fool with fools all this time, but that law existed for me and for all; that to me belonged trust, a child's trust and obedience, and the worship of ideas, and I should never be fool more. Well, in the space of an hour, probably, I was let down from this height; I was at my old tricks, the selfish member of a selfish society. My life is superficial, takes no root in the deep world; I ask, When shall I die, and be relieved of the responsibility of seeing an Universe which I do not use? I wish to exchange this flash-of-lightning faith for continuous daylight, this fever-glow for a benign climate.

—THE TRANSCENDENTALIST

Have you had "a certain brief experience" that surprised you? Have you wished you could exchange such "flash-of-lightening" experiences for "continuous daylight"?

OCTOBER 11

There is a relation between the hours of our life and the centuries of time. As the air I breathe is drawn from the great repositories of nature, as the light on my book is yielded by a star a hundred millions of miles distant, as the poise of my body depends on the equilibrium of centrifugal and centripetal forces, so the hours should be instructed by the ages, and the ages explained by the hours. Of the universal mind each individual man is one more incarnation. All its properties consist in him. Each new fact in his private experience flashes a light on what great bodies of men have done, and the crises of his life refer to national crises. Every revolution was first a thought in one man's mind, and when the same thought occurs to another man, it is the key to that era. Every reform was once a private opinion, and when it shall be a private opinion again, it will solve the problem of the age.

—HISTORY

Do the properties of the universal mind reside in you? How does that make you related to everyone else?

OCTOBER 12

Conversation is a game of circles. In conversation we pluck up the *termini* which bound the common of silence on every side. The parties are not to be judged by the spirit they partake and even express under this Pentecost. Tomorrow they will have receded from this high-water mark. Tomorrow you shall find them stooping under the old pack-saddles. Yet let us enjoy the cloven flame whilst it glows on our walls. When each new speaker strikes a new light, emancipates us from the oppression of the last speaker, to oppress us with the greatness and exclusiveness of his own thought, then yields us to another redeemer, we seem to recover our rights, to become men. O, what truths profound and executable only in ages and orbs are supposed in the announcement of every truth!

—CIRCLES

Do you find conversation exhilarating? Has conversation made a high-water mark in your spiritual life?

OCTOBER 13

Akin to the benefit of foreign travel, the aesthetic value of rail-
roads is to unite the advantages of town and country life, neither of which we can spare. A man should live in or near a
large town, because, let his own genius be what it may, it will
repel quite as much of agreeable and valuable talent as it draws,
and, in a city, the total attraction of all the citizens is sure to
conquer, first or last, every repulsion, and drag the most im-
probable hermit within its walls some day in the year. In town,
he can find the swimming-school, the gymnasium, the danc-
ing-master, the shooting-gallery, opera, theater, and panorama;
the chemist's shop, the museum of natural history, the gal-
lery of fine arts, the national orators, in their turn, foreign
travellers, the libraries, and his club. In the country, he
can find solitude and reading, manly labor, cheap living,
and his old shoes; moors for game, hills for geology, and
groves for devotion.

—CULTURE

---

*Do you feel more at home in the town or in the country?
Have you tried to achieve a balance between them both?*

OCTOBER 14

It was a poetic attempt to lift this mountain of Fate, to reconcile this despotism of race with liberty, which led the Hindoos to say, "Fate is nothing but the deeds committed in a prior state of existence." I find the coincidence of the extremes of eastern and western speculation in the daring statement of Schelling, "there is in every man a certain feeling, that he has been what he is from all eternity, and by no means became such in time." To say it less sublimely,—in the history of the individual is always an account of his condition, and he knows himself to be a party to his present estate.

—FATE

Do you believe in karma or predestination? How do you "attempt to lift this mountain of Fate"?

The old fable covers a doctrine ever new and sublime; that there is One Man,—present to all particular men only partially, or through one faculty; and that you must take the whole society to find the whole man. Man is not a farmer, or a professor, or an engineer, but he is all. Man is priest, and scholar, and statesman, and producer, and soldier. In the divided or social state, these functions are parceled out to individuals, each of whom aims to do his stint of the joint work, whilst each other performs his. The fable implies, that the individual, to possess himself, must sometimes return from his own labor to embrace all the other laborers. But unfortunately, this original unit, this fountain of power, has been so distributed to multitudes, has been so minutely subdivided and peddled out, that it is spilled into drops, and cannot be gathered. The state of society is one in which the members have suffered amputation from the trunk, and strut about so many walking monsters,—a good finger, a neck, a stomach, an elbow, but never a man.

—THE AMERICAN SCHOLAR

Do you think people lack wholeness? What would it take to be a whole person?

And this is the progress of every earnest mind; from the works of man and the activity of the hands to a delight in the faculties which rule them; from a respect to the works to a wise wonder at this mystic element of time in which he is conditioned; from local skills and the economy which reckons the amount of production *per* hour to the finer economy which respects the quality of what is done, and the right we have to the work, or the fidelity with which it flows from ourselves; then to the depth of thought it betrays, looking to its universality, or that its roots are in eternity, not in time. Then it flows from character, that sublime health which values one moment as another, and makes us great in all conditions, and as the only definition we have of freedom and power.

— Works and Days

Have you progressed as an "earnest mind"? Have you practiced "the finer economy" that Emerson describes?

OCTOBER 17

Is the ideal society always to be only a dream, a song, a luxury of thought and never a step taken to realise the vision for living and indigent men without misgiving within and wildest ridicule abroad? Between poetry and prose must the great gulf yawn ever and they who try to bridge it over be lunatics or hypocrites? And yet the too dark ground of history is starred over with solitary heroes who dared to believe better of their brothers, and who prevailed by actually executing the law (the high ideal) in their own life, and though a hissing and an offence to their contemporaries yet they became a celestial sign to all succeeding souls as they journeyed through nature. How shines the names of Abraham, Diogenes, Pythagoras, and the transcendent Jesus, in antiquity! And now, in our turn, shall we esteem the elegant decorum of our world, and what is called greatness and splendor in it, of such a vast and outweighing worth, as to reckon all aspirations after the Better, fanciful or pitiable; and all aspirants pert and loathsome? There is a limit, and, (as in some hours, we fancy,) a pretty speedy limit, to the value of what is called success in life. The great world too always bears unexpected witness to the rhapsodies of the idealists.

—JOURNAL, 1838

Do you consider yourself an idealist in Emerson's sense of the term? Do you ever feel discouraged in your idealism?

Instinct is our name for the potential wit. Each man has a feeling that what is done anywhere is done by the same wit as his. All men are his representatives, and he is glad to see that his wit can work at this or that problem as it ought to be done, and better than he could do it. We feel as if one man wrote all the books, painted, built, in dark ages; and we are sure that it can do more than ever was done. It was the same mind that built the world. That is Instinct. Ask what the Instinct declares, and we have little to say. He is no newsmonger, no disputant, no talker. 'T is a taper, a spark in the great night. Yet a spark at which all the illuminations of human arts and sciences were kindled. This is that glimpse of indistinguishable light by which men are guided; though it does not show objects, yet it shows the way. This is that sense by which men feel when they are wronged, though they do not see how. This is that source of thought and feeling which acts on masses of men, on all men at certain times with resistless power. Ever at intervals leaps a word or fact to light which is no man's invention, but the common instinct, making the revolutions that never go back.

—NATURAL HISTORY OF INTELLECT

Have you exercised your instinct or intuition in making a decision? Can you trust your instincts and intuitions?

OCTOBER 19

Books are the best of things, well used; abused, among the worst. What is the right use? What is the one end, which all means go to effect? They are for nothing but to inspire. I had better never see a book, than to be warped by its attraction clean out of my own orbit, and made a satellite instead of a system. The one thing in the world, of value, is the active soul. This every man is entitled to; this every man contains within him, although, in almost all men, obstructed, and as yet unborn. The soul active sees absolute truth; and utters truth, or creates. In this action, it is genius; not the privilege of here and there a favorite, but the sound estate of every man. In its essence, it is progressive. The book, the college, the school of art, the institution of any kind, stop with some past utterance of genius. This is good, say they,—let us hold by this. They pin me down. They look backward and not forward. But genius looks forward: the eyes of man are set in his forehead, not in his hindhead: man hopes: genius creates.

— THE AMERICAN SCHOLAR

Can you think of a book that inspired you? Is reading part of your spiritual practice?

OCTOBER 20

Our moral nature is vitiated by any interference of our will. People represent virtue as a struggle, and take to themselves great airs upon their attainments, and the question is everywhere vexed, when a noble nature is commended, whether the man is not better who strives with temptation. But there is no merit in the matter. Either God is there, or he is not there. We love characters in proportion as they are impulsive and spontaneous. The less a man thinks or knows about his virtues, the better we like him.... When we see a soul whose acts are all regal, graceful, and pleasant as roses, we must thank God that such things can be and are.

—Spiritual Laws

Are people impulsively good? Do you know people who are naturally virtuous?

OCTOBER 21

Well, we are all the children of genius, the children of virtue,—and feel their inspirations in our happier hours. Is not every man sometimes a radical in politics? Men are conservatives when they are least vigorous, or when they are most luxurious. They are conservatives after dinner, or before taking their rest; when they are sick, or aged: in the morning, or when their intellect or their conscience have been aroused, when they hear music, or when they read poetry, they are radicals. In the circle of the rankest tories that could be collected in England, Old or New, let a powerful and stimulating intellect, a man of great heart and mind, act on them, and very quickly these frozen conservators will yield to the friendly influence, these hopeless will begin to hope, these haters will begin to love, these immovable statues will begin to spin and revolve.

—NEW ENGLAND REFORMERS

Are you more often a conservative or a radical? Do you believe in the ability of "powerful and stimulating intellect" to radicalize people? Can you think of instances of this in your experience?

OCTOBER 22

Why should I hasten to solve every riddle which life offers me? I am well assured that the Questioner, who brings me so many problems, will bring the answers also in due time. Very rich, very potent, very cheerful Giver that he is, he shall have it all his own way, for me. Why should I give up my thought, because I cannot answer an objection to it? Consider only, whether it remains in my life the same it was. That only which we have within, can we see without. If we meet no gods, it is because we harbor none. If there is grandeur in you, you will find grandeur in porters and sweeps. He only is rightly immortal, to whom all things are immortal. I have read somewhere, that none is accomplished, so long as any are incomplete; that the happiness of one cannot consist with the misery of any other.

— WORSHIP

Do you harbor any gods? Do you see any? Is there grandeur in you? Do you see it in others? Are you whole "so long as any are incomplete"?

I take it to be a main end of that education which the world works for each soul, to touch the springs of wonder in us, and make us alive to the mystery to which we are born. That done, all is well begun. And the high miracles of the human estate begin with the act of reason. And I shall think the hour of meditation cannot be more wisely spent than in accosting a few of the miracles, the points of astonishment, the occasions of wise admiration that shine in our common experience.

—MORAL SENSE

Has your own education ever touched "the springs of wonder" in you? Can meditation be a part of your spiritual practice?

OCTOBER 24

It is a peculiarity... of humour in me, my strong propensity for strolling. I deliberately shut up my books in a cloudy July noon, put on my old clothes and old hat and slink away to the whortleberry bushes and slip with the greatest satisfaction into a little cow path where I am sure I can defy observation. This point gained, I solace myself for hours with picking blue berries and other trash of the woods far from fame behind the birch trees. I seldom enjoy hours as I do these. I remember them in winter; I expect them in spring. I do not know a creature that I think has the same humour or would think it respectable.

—JOURNAL, 1828

Do you have a "propensity for strolling"? How would you describe the satisfaction you derive from it?

Ah ye old ghosts! ye builders of dungeons in the air! why do I ever allow you to encroach on me a moment; a moment to win me to your hapless company? In every week there is some hour when I read my commission in every cipher of nature, and know that I was made for another office, a professor of the Joyous Science, a detector and delineator of occult harmonies and unpublished beauties, a herald of civility, nobility, learning, and wisdom; an affirmer of the One Law, yet as one who should affirm it in music or dancing, a priest of the Soul yet one who would better love to celebrate it through the beauty of health and harmonious power.

—JOURNAL, 1841

How would you describe the "office" for which you were made? What do you affirm and how do you affirm it?

OCTOBER 26

Sixty years ago, the books read, the sermons and prayers heard, the habits of thought of religious persons, were all directed on death.... The emphasis of all the good books given to young people was on death. We were all taught that we were born to die; and over that, all the terrors that theology could gather from savage nations were added to increase the gloom. A great change has occurred. Death is seen as a natural event, and is met with firmness. A wise man in our time caused to be written on his tomb, "Think on living." That inscription describes a progress in opinion. Cease from this antedating of your experience. Sufficient to today are the duties of today. Don't waste life in doubts and fears; spend yourself on the work before you, well assured that the right performance of this hour's duties will be the best preparation for the hours or ages that follow it:—
"The name of death was never terrible to him that knew how to live."

—IMMORTALITY

What is your view of death? Do you know how to live?

Few have overheard the gods, or surprised their secret. Life is a succession of lessons which must be lived to be understood. All is riddle, and the key to a riddle is another riddle. There are as many pillows of illusion as flakes in a snow-storm. We wake from one dream into another dream. The toys, to be sure, are various, and are graduated in refinement to the quality of the dupe. The intellectual man requires a fine bait; the sots are easily amused. But everybody is drugged with his own frenzy, and the pageant marches at all hours, with music and banner and badge.

—ILLUSIONS

What "lessons" have you learned? What "toys" have distracted you?

OCTOBER 28

Daughters of Time, the hypocritic Days,
Muffled and dumb like barefoot dervishes,
And marching single in an endless file,
Bring diadems and fagots in their hands.
To each they offer gifts after his will,
Bread, kingdoms, stars and sky that holds them all.
I, in my pleachéd garden, watched the pomp,
Forgot my morning wishes, hastily
Took a few herbs and apples, and the Day
Turned and departed silent. I, too late,
Under her solemn fillet saw the scorn.

—Days

---

*What are some of the gifts the days bring to you? Have you
ever refused them and later regretted it?*

Fortune, Minerva, Muse, Holy Ghost,—these are quaint names, too narrow to cover this unbounded substance. The baffled intellect must still kneel before this cause, which refuses to be named,—ineffable cause, which every fine genius has essayed to represent by some emphatic symbol, as, Thales by water, Anaximenes by air, Anaxagoras by (Nous) thought, Zoroaster by fire, Jesus and the moderns by love: and the metaphor of each has become a national religion. The Chinese Mencius has not been the least successful in his generalization. "I fully understand language," he said, "and nourish well my vast-flowing vigor."—"I beg to ask what you call vast-flowing vigor?"—said his companion. "The explanation," replied Mencius, "is difficult. This vigor is supremely great, and in the highest degree unbending. Nourish it correctly, and do it no injury, and it will fill up the vacancy between heaven and earth. This vigor accords with and assists justice and reason, and leaves no hunger."—In our more correct writing, we give to this generalization the name of Being, and thereby confess that we have arrived as far as we can go. Suffice it for the joy of the universe, that we have not arrived at a wall, but at interminable oceans. Our life seems not present, so much as prospective; not for the affairs on which it is wasted, but as a hint of this vast-flowing vigor. Most of life seems to be mere advertisement of faculty: information is given us not to sell ourselves cheap; that we are very great.

— EXPERIENCE

What names do you give to the "unbounded substance that the world's great thinkers have tried to represent by some emphatic symbol"? Have you ever felt that you stand on the verge of "this vast-flowing vigor"?

Man does not live by bread alone, but by faith, by admiration, by sympathy. 'T is very shallow to say that cotton, or iron, or silver and gold are kings of the world; there are rulers that will at any moment make these forgotten. Fear will. Love will. Character will. Men live by their credence. Governments stand by it,—by the faith that the people share,—whether it comes from the religion in which they were bred, or from an original conscience in themselves, which the popular religion echoes. If government could only stand by force, if the instinct of the people was to resist the government, it is plain that the government must be two to one in order to be secure, and then it would not be safe from desperate individuals. But no; the old commandment, "Thou shalt not kill," holds down New York, and London, and Paris, and not a police or horse-guards.

— THE SOVEREIGNTY OF ETHICS

What keeps morality in place? Do you believe in yourself?

Concert is neither better nor worse, neither more nor less potent than individual force. All the men in the world cannot make a statue walk and speak, cannot make a drop of blood, or a blade of grass, any more than one man can. But let there be one man, let there be truth in two men, in ten men, then is concert for the first time possible, because the force which moves the world is a new quality, and can never be furnished by adding whatever qualities of a different kind. What is the use of the concert of the false and the disunited? There can be no concert in two, where there is no concert in one. When the individual is not *individual* but is dual; when his thoughts look one way, and his reactions another; when his faith is traversed by his habits; when his will, enlightened by reason, is warped by his sense; when with one hand he rows, and with the other backs water, what concert can be?

—New England Reformers

Can group action be effective if people are "false and disunited" within themselves? Can it fail if people have integrity?

NOVEMBER

Meditations

NOVEMBER 1

The universe is a more amazing puzzle than ever as you glance along this bewildering series of animated forms,—the hazy butterflies, the carved shells, the birds, beasts, fishes, insects, snakes,—and the upheaving principle of life everywhere incipient, in the very rock aping organized forms. Not a form so grotesque, so savage, nor so beautiful but is an expression of some property inherent in man the observer,—an occult relation between the very scorpions and man. I feel the centipede in me—cayman, carp, eagle, and fox. I am moved by strange sympathies, I say continually "I will be a naturalist."

—JOURNAL, 1833
[on a visit to the *Jardin des Plantes* in Paris.]

Do you feel a kinship with the plants and animals? Do you sense "an occult relation" between "scorpions and man"?

All the comfort I have found teaches me to confide that I shall not have less in times and places that I do not yet know. I have known admirable persons, without feeling that they exhaust the possibilities of virtue and talent. I have seen what glories of climate, of summer mornings and evenings, of midnight sky; I have enjoyed the benefits of all this complex machinery of arts and civilization, and its results of comfort. The good Power can easily provide me millions more as good. Shall I hold on with both hands to every paltry possession? All I have seen teaches me to trust the Creator for all I have not seen. Whatever it be which the great Providence prepares for us, it must be something large and generous, and in the great style of his works. The future must be up to the style of our faculties,—of memory, or hope, of imagination, of reason. I have a house, a closet which holds my books, a table, a garden, a field: are these, any or all, a reason for refusing the angel who beckons me away,— as if there were no room or skill elsewhere that could reproduce for me as my like or my enlarging wants may require? We wish to live for what is great, not for what is mean. I do not wish to live for the sake of my warm house, my orchard, or my pictures. I do not wish to live to wear out my boots.

—IMMORTALITY

Do you have confidence in what providence has in store for you? What do you live for?

[Of the successful.] Their success lay in their parallelism to the course of thought, which found in them an unobstructed channel; and the wonders of which they were the visible conductors seemed to the eye their deed. Did the wires generate the galvanism? It is even true that there was less in them on which they could reflect, than in another; as the virtue of a pipe is to be smooth and hollow. That which externally seemed will and immovableness was willingness and self-annihilation. Could Shakespeare give a theory of Shakespeare? Could ever a man of prodigious mathematical genius convey to others any insight into his methods? If he could communicate that secret, it would instantly lose its exaggerated value, blending with the daylight and the vital energy the power to stand and to go.

—Spiritual Laws

Are you able to be a conduit for creativity? Is there something spontaneous about genius?

NOVEMBER 4

We cannot trifle with this reality, this cropping-out in our planted gardens of the core of the world. No picture of life can have any veracity that does not admit the odious facts. A man's power is hooped in by a necessity, which, by many experiments, he touches on every side, until he learns its arc. The element running through entire nature, which we popularly call Fate, is known to us as limitation. Whatever limits us, we call Fate. If we are brute and barbarous, the fate takes a brute and dreadful shape. As we refine, our checks become finer. If we rise to spiritual culture, the antagonism takes a spiritual form. In the Hindoo fables, Vishnu follows Maya through all her ascending changes, from insect and crawfish up to elephant; whatever form she took, he took the male form of that kind, until she became at last woman and goddess, and he a man and a god. The limitations refine as the soul purifies, but the ring of necessity is always perched at the top.

—FATE

How does your philosophy of life account for "the odious facts" of existence? What conditions limit you?

NOVEMBER 5

Excite the soul, and it becomes suddenly virtuous. Touch the deep heart, and all these listless, stingy, beef-eating bystanders will see the dignity of a sentiment; will say, This is good, and all I have I will give for that. Excite the soul, and the weather and the town and your condition in the world will all disappear; the world itself loses its solidity, nothing remains but the soul and the Divine Presence in which it lives.

—JOURNAL, 1835

Can you remember a time when your soul was excited? What did that feel like? Did "your condition in the world" disappear?

NOVEMBER 6

The main interest which any aspects of the Times can have for us, is the great spirit which gazes through them, the light which they can shed on the wonderful questions, What we are? and Whither we tend? We do not wish to be deceived. Here we drift, like white sail across the wild ocean, now bright on the wave, now darkling in the trough of the sea;—but from what port did we sail? Who knows? Or to what port are we bound? Who knows? There is no one to tell us but such poor weather-tossed mariners as ourselves, whom we speak as we pass, or who have hoisted some signal, or floated to us some letter in a bottle from far. But what know they more than we? They also found themselves on this wondrous sea. No; from the older sailors, nothing. Over all their speaking-trumpets, the gray sea and the loud winds answer, Not in us; not in Time. Where then but in Ourselves, where but in that Thought through which we communicate with absolute nature, and are made aware that, whilst we shed the dust of which we are built, grain by grain, till it is all gone, the law which clothes us with humanity remains new? where, but in the intuitions which are vouchsafed us from within, shall we learn the Truth?... Underneath all these appearances, lies that which is, that which lives, that which causes. This ever renewing generation of appearances rests on a reality, and a reality that is alive.

— Introductory Lecture on the Times

What is your view of the times we live in? Do you ask yourself "Where we are? and Whither we tend?" Do you agree with Emerson that the answers lie within?

NOVEMBER 7

The whole world is in conspiracy against itself in religious matters. The best experience is beggarly when compared with the
immense possibilities of man. Divine as the life of Jesus is, what
an outrage to represent it as tantamount to the Universe! To
seize one accidental good man that happened to exist somewhere at some time and say to the new born soul, Behold thy
pattern; aim no longer to possess entire Nature, to fill the horizon, to fill the infinite amplitude of being with great life, to be
in sympathy and in relation with all creatures, to lose all pri-
vateness by sharing all natural action, shining with the Day,
undulating with the Sea, growing with the tree, instinctive
with the animals, entranced in beatific vision with the human
reason. Renounce a life so broad and deep as a pretty dream
and go in the harness of that past individual, assume his manners, speak his speech,—this is the madness of christendom.

—JOURNAL, 1839

---

*Do you think the world "is in conspiracy against itself in
religious matters"? Does Jesus take up too much of the
spiritual horizon, so to speak?*

NOVEMBER 8

When, at last, that which we have always longed for, is arrived, and shines on us with glad rays out of that far celestial land, then to be coarse, then to be critical, and treat such a visitant with the jabber and suspicion of the streets, argues a vulgarity that seems to shut the doors of heaven. Is there any religion but this, to know, that, wherever in the wide desert of being, the holy sentiment we cherish has opened into a flower, it blooms for me? If none sees it, I see it; I am aware, if I alone, of the greatness of the fact. Whilst it blooms, I will keep Sabbath or holy time, and suspend my gloom, and my folly and jokes. Nature is indulged by the presence of this guest.

—CHARACTER

Has the spirit flowered for you? Emerson believes that this is true religion. Would you agree?

NOVEMBER 9

The same Omniscience flows into the intellect, and makes what we call genius.... But genius is religious. It is a larger imbibing of the common heart. It is not anomalous, but more like, and not less like other men. There is, in all great poets, a wisdom of humanity which is superior to any talents they exercise.... This energy does not descend into individual life on any other condition than entire possession. It comes to the lowly and simple; it comes to whomsoever will put off what is foreign and proud; it comes as insight; it comes as serenity and grandeur.... The soul that ascends to worship the great God is plain and true; has no rose-color, no fine friends, no chivalry, no adventures; does not want admiration; dwells in the hour that now is, in the earnest experience of the common day,—by reason of the present moment and the mere trifle having become porous to thought, and bibulous of the sea of light.

—THE OVER-SOUL

Have you known people with genius in Emerson's sense of the word? What does it mean to be "plain and true"?

We are natural believers. Truth, or the connection between cause and effect, alone interests us. We are persuaded that a thread runs through all things: all worlds are strung on it, as beads; and men, and events, and life, come to us only because of that thread; they pass and repass only that we may know the direction and continuity of that line. A book or statement which goes to show that there is no line, but random and chaos, a calamity out of nothing, a prosperity and no account of it, a hero born from a fool, a fool from a hero,—dispirits us. Seen or unseen, we believe the tie exists. Talent makes counterfeit ties; genius finds the real ones.

—MONTAIGNE; OR, THE SKEPTIC

Do you agree with Emerson that we are natural believers, that religion is innate? Does a thread run through all things, or is all random and chaos?

NOVEMBER 11

Books are for the scholar's idle times. When he can read God directly, the hour is too precious to be wasted in other men's transcripts of their readings. But when the intervals of darkness come, as come they must,—when the sun is hid, and the stars withdraw their shining,—we repair to the lamps which were kindled by their ray, to guide our steps to the East again, where the dawn is. We hear, that we may speak.

—THE AMERICAN SCHOLAR

When can you "read God directly"? Do you set that time aside for spiritual practice? Do you agree that "We hear, that we may speak"?

NOVEMBER 12

I am not careful to justify myself. I own I am gladdened by seeing the predominance of the saccharine principle throughout vegetable nature, and not less by beholding in morals that unrestrained inundation of the principle of good into every chink and hole that selfishness has left open, yea, into selfishness and sin itself; so that no evil is pure, nor hell itself without its extreme satisfactions. But lest I should mislead any when I have my own head and obey my whims, let me remind the reader that I am only an experimenter. Do not set the least value on what I do, or the least discredit on what I do not, as if I pretended to settle any thing as true or false. I unsettle all things. No facts are to me sacred; none are profane; I simply experiment, an endless seeker, with no Past at my back.

—Circles

Do you frequently feel compelled to justify yourself? Do you consider yourself an experimenter, "an endless seeker"?

NOVEMBER 13

The word miracle, as it is used, only indicates the ignorance of the devotee, staring with wonder to see water turned into wine, and heedless of the stupendous fact of his own personality. Here he stands, a lonely thought harmoniously organized into correspondence with the universe of mind and matter. What narrative of wonders coming down from a thousand years ought to charm his attention like this? Certainly it is human to value a general consent, a fraternity of believers, a crowded church; but as the sentiment purifies and rises, it leaves crowds. It makes churches of two, churches of one. A fatal disservice does this Swedenborg or other who offers to do my thinking for me. It seems as if, when the Spirit of God speaks so plainly to each soul, it were an impiety to be listening to one or another saint. Jesus was better than others, because he refused to listen to others and listened at home.

—THE SOVEREIGNTY OF ETHICS

How do you define a miracle? Have you ever experienced one?

NOVEMBER 14

The moral must be the measure of health. If your eye is on the eternal, your intellect will grow, and your opinions and actions will have a beauty which no learning or combined advantages of other men can rival. The moment of your loss of faith, and acceptance of the lucrative standard, will be marked in the pause, or solstice of genius, the sequent retrogression, and the inevitable loss of attraction to other minds. The vulgar are sensible of the change in you, and of your descent, though they clap you on the back, and congratulate you on your increased common sense.

—WORSHIP

Is it difficult to keep your eye on the eternal? Is it difficult to resist "the lucrative standard"?

NOVEMBER 15

And yet we do not provide for the greatest good of life. We take care of our health; we lay up money; we make our roof tight, and our clothing sufficient; but who provides wisely that he shall not be wanting in the best property of all,—friends?... It makes no difference, in looking back five years, how you have been dieted or dressed; whether you have been lodged on the first floor or the attic; whether you have had gardens and baths, good cattle and horses, have been carried in a neat equipage, or in a ridiculous truck: these things are forgotten so quickly, and leave no effect. But it counts much whether we have had good companions, in that time;—almost as much as what we have been doing.

—CONSIDERATIONS BY THE WAY

Whom do you count among your companions? What do you look for in a friend?

We cannot write the order of the variable winds. How can we penetrate the law of our shifting moods and susceptibility? Yet they differ as all and nothing. Instead of the firmament of yesterday, which our eyes require, it is today an eggshell which coops us in; we cannot even see what or where our stars of destiny are. From day to day, the capital facts of human life are hidden from our eyes. Suddenly the mist rolls up, and reveals them, and we think how much good time is gone, that might have been saved, had any hint of these things been shown. A sudden rise in the road shows us the system of mountains, and all the summits, which have been just as near us all the year, but quite out of mind.

—ILLUSIONS

Are there times when the fog of illusion lifts for you? What are "the capital facts of human life"?

NOVEMBER 17

On its own level, or in view of nature, temperament is final. I see not, if one be once caught in this trap of so-called sciences, any escape for the man from the links of the chain of physical necessity. Given such an embryo, such a history must follow. On this platform, one lives in a sty of sensualism, and would soon come to suicide. But it is impossible that the creative power should exclude itself. Into every intelligence there is a door which is never closed, through which the creator passes. The intellect, seeker of absolute truth, or the heart, lover of absolute good, intervenes for our succor, and at one whisper of these high powers, we awake from ineffectual struggles with this nightmare. We hurl it into its own hell, and cannot again contract ourselves to so base a state.

— EXPERIENCE

Is temperament final? Can people alter their temperament and outlook on life?

Friendship requires that rare mean betwixt likeness and unlikeness, that piques each with the presence of power and of consent in the other party. Let me be alone to the end of the world, rather than that my friend should overstep, by a word or a look, his real sympathy. I am equally balked by antagonism and by compliance. Let him not cease an instant to be himself. The only joy I have in his being mine, is that the not mine is mine. I hate, where I looked for a manly furtherance, or at least a manly resistance, to find a mush of concession. Better to be a nettle in the side of your friend than his echo. The condition which high friendship demands is ability to do without it. That high office requires great and sublime parts. There must be very two, before there can be very one. Let it be an alliance of two large, formidable natures, mutually beheld, mutually feared, before yet they recognize the deep identity which beneath these disparities unites them.

— FRIENDSHIP

Do you value the friend who is honest with you? Do you have friends who will tell you what they think rather than what you want to hear?

NOVEMBER 19

The Teacher is teaching but has not finished his word. That word never will be finished. It was before the heavens and shall be after them. But a part of this message is spoken this day and every day. There are truths now being revealed. There is a revolution of religious opinion taking effect around us, it seems to me the greatest of all revolutions which have ever occurred, that, namely, which has separated the individual from the whole world and made him demand a faith satisfactory to his own proper nature, whose full extent he now contemplates. A little while ago men were supposed to be saved or lost as one race; Adam was the federal head and, in books of theology, his sin was a federal sin which cut off the hopes of all his posterity. The atoning blood of Christ, again, was a sacrifice for all, by which the divine vengeance was averted from you and me. But now, men have begun to feel and to inquire for their several sake in the joy and the suffering of the whole. What is my relation to Almighty God? What is my relation to my fellow man? What am I designed for? What are my duties? What is my destiny? The soul peremptorily asks these questions— the Whence and the Why—and refuses to be put off with insufficient answers.

—SERMON 165

Are you satisfied with the answers that "books of theology" give to the big questions of life, or do you feel the need to answer those questions for yourself? Are we in the midst of a religious revolution?

Here again, as so often, nature delights to put us between extreme antagonisms, and our safety is in the skill with which we keep the diagonal line. Solitude is impractical, and society fatal. We must keep our head in the one and our hands in the other. The conditions are met, if we keep our independence, yet do not lose our sympathy. These wonderful horses need to be driven by fine hands. We require such a solitude as shall hold us to its revelations when we are in the street and in palaces.

—SOCIETY AND SOLITUDE

Have you tried to keep "the diagonal line" between society and solitude? What do you do to practice solitude in your life?

But when, following the invisible steps of thought, we come to inquire, Whence is matter? and Whereto? many truths arise to us out of the recesses of consciousness. We learn that the highest is present to the soul of man, that the dread universal essence, which is not wisdom, or love, or beauty, or power, but all in one, and each entirely, is that for which all things exist, and that by which they are; that spirit creates; that behind nature, throughout nature, spirit is present; one and not compound, it does not act upon us from without, that is, in space and time, but spiritually, or through ourselves: therefore, that spirit, that is, the Supreme Being, does not build up nature around us, but puts it forth through us, as the life of the tree puts forth new branches and leaves through the pores of the old. As a plant upon the earth, so a man rests on the bosom of God; he is nourished by unfailing fountains, and draws, at his need, inexhaustible power. Who can set bounds to the possibility of man? Once inhale the upper air, being admitted to behold the absolute natures of justice and truth, and we learn that man has access to the entire mind of the Creator, is himself the creator in the finite.

—NATURE

Does your experience of nature invigorate you and make you feel powerful? Does it make you feel related "to the entire mind of the Creator"?

Whenever therefore a soul is true, is simple, and expelling all wilfulness consents to God, and receives the Soul of the Soul into itself, then old things pass away, then means, teachers, texts, temples, fall; it lives Now, and not from the Past.... The present hour is the descending God, and all things obey: all the past exists to it as subordinate: all the future is contained in it. All things are made sacred by relation to it,—one thing as much as another. It smooths down the mountainous differences of appearance, and breathes one life through creation from side to side. All things are dissolved to their centre by the glory of the Cause, and therefore in the Universal miracle, petty and particular miracles disappear. This is and must be. Do not therefore be deceived by any false annunciations of the presence of God. If a man claims to know and speak of God and carries you backward to the phraseology of some old mouldered nation in another country in another world, believe him not: he does not speak for God: God does not speak to him.

—JOURNAL, 1838

Have you ever felt that "the present hour is the descending God"? Do you still look to "the phraseology of some old mouldered nation" for knowledge of God?

NOVEMBER 23

It is very unhappy, but too late to be helped, the discovery we have made, that we exist. That discovery is called the Fall of Man. Ever afterwards, we suspect our instruments. We have learned that we do not see directly, but mediately, and that we have no means of correcting these colored and distorting lenses which we are, or of computing the amount of their errors. Perhaps these subject-lenses have a creative power; perhaps there are no objects. Once we lived in what we saw; now, the rapaciousness of this new power, which threatens to absorb all things, engages us. Nature, art, persons, letters, religions,— objects, successively tumble in, and God is but one of its ideas. Nature and literature are subjective phenomena; every evil and every good thing is a shadow which we cast.

—EXPERIENCE

Does self-consciousness lead to self-doubt? Do you believe that "every evil and every good thing is a shadow which we cast"?

NOVEMBER 24

What is this intoxicating sentiment, that allies this scrap of dust to the whole of Nature, and the whole of Fate? that makes this doll a dweller in Ages, mocker at Time, able to spurn all outward advantages; peer and master of the elements? I am taught by it, that, what touches any thread in the vast web of being touches me. I am representative of the Whole, and the good of the Whole, or, what I call the Right,—makes me invulnerable. Crush me in a mortar, pound me to powder, destroy my name and vestige out of earth, and I rise unhurt: Fire cannot burn, nor seas drown, nor tempests blow away this holy dream. How came this creation so magically woven, that nothing can do me mischief but myself? that an invisible fence surrounds my being, which screens me from all harm that I will to resist? that we pass for what we are; that we do not live by times, but by qualities; that the evils we suffer are the just measures of those we have done? If I will stand upright, the creation cannot bend me. But if I violate myself, if I commit a crime, the lightening loiters by the speed of retribution, and every act is not hereafter, but instantaneously rewarded according to its quality. It seemed to me an impiety to be listening to one and another saint, when the pure heaven was pouring itself into each one of us on the simple condition of obedience. To listen to any second-hand Gospel is perdition of the First Gospel,—that is, your own.

— THE RULE OF LIFE

How would you describe the "intoxicating element" that allies us to nature and to fate? Do you agree with Emerson that the good of the whole makes us invulnerable? How so?

The Religion that is afraid of science dishonors God and commits suicide. It acknowledges that it is not equal to the whole of truth, that it legislates, tyrannizes over a village of God's empire, but is not the immutable universal law. Every influx of atheism, of skepticism, is thus made useful as a mercury pill assaulting and removing a diseased religion and making way for truth.... Keep the soul always turned to God. Nothing so vast but feel that he contains it. Let nothing be so real or pure or grand as He is. If your idea of him is dim or perplexed, pray and think and act more. It is the education of the soul. It is the sure way of individual increase. Sincerity is always holy, and always strong. Come good or ill, the pure in heart are in the right way. And presently and often, you shall be rewarded with clearer perception, the sense of more intimate communion.

—JOURNAL, 1831

Does skepticism play a role in your religious life? Are you able to reconcile science with a belief in God?

NOVEMBER 26

The history of mankind is the history of arrested growth. This premature stop, I know not how, befalls most of us in early youth; as if the growth of high powers, the access to rare truths, closed at two or three years in the child, while all the pagan faculties went ripening on to sixty. So long as you are capable of advance, so long as you have not abdicated the hope and future of a divine soul. That wonderful oracle will reply when it is consulted, and there is no history or tradition, no rule of life or art or science, on which it is not a competent and the only competent judge. Man was made for conflict, not for rest. In action is his power; not in his goals but in his transitions man is great. Instantly he is dwarfed by self-indulgence. The truest state of mind rested in becomes false.

—NATURAL HISTORY OF INTELLECT

What role has conflict played in your thinking? What is the relationship between conflict and growth?

And so in relation to that future hour, that spectre clothed with beauty at our curtain by night, at our table by day,—the apprehension, the assurance of a coming change. The race of mankind have always offered at least this implied thanks for the gift of existence,—namely, the terror of its being taken away; the insatiable curiosity and appetite for its continuation. The whole revelation that is vouchsafed us, is, the gentle trust, which, in our experience we find, will cover also with flowers the slopes of this chasm. Of immortality, the soul, when well employed, is incurious. It is so well, that it is sure it will be well. It asks no questions of the Supreme Power. . . . Higher than the question of our duration is the question of our deserving. Immortality will come to such as are fit for it, and he who would be a great soul in future, must be a great soul now.

— WORSHIP

What is your view of immortality? How would one be fit for immortality?

The world globes itself in a drop of dew.... So do we put our life into every act. The true doctrine of omnipresence is, that God reappears with all his parts in every moss and cobweb. The value of the universe contrives to throw itself into every point. If the good is there, so is the evil; if the affinity, so the repulsion; if the force, so the limitation. Thus is the universe alive. All things are moral. That soul, which within us is a sentiment, outside of us is a law.... Justice is not postponed. A perfect equity adjusts its balance in all parts of life.... Every secret is told, every crime is punished, every virtue rewarded, every wrong redressed, in silence and certainty. What we call retribution is the universal necessity by which the whole appears wherever a part appears.

—COMPENSATION

Do you see God in "every moss and cobweb"? What does "All things are moral" mean?

Virtue is the adherence in action to the nature of things, and the nature of things makes it prevalent. It consists in a perpetual substitution of being for seeming, and with sublime propriety God is described as saying, *I am.* The lesson which these observations convey is, Be, and not seem. Let us acquiesce. Let us take our bloated nothingness out of the path of the divine circuits. Let us unlearn our wisdom of the world. Let us lie low in the Lord's power, and learn that truth alone makes rich and great. If you visit your friend, why need you apologize for not having visited him, and waste his time and deface your own act? Visit him now. Let him feel that the highest love has come to see him, in thee its lowest organ. Or why need you torment yourself and friend by secret self-reproaches that you have not assisted him or complimented him with gifts and salutations heretofore? Be a gift and a benediction. Shine with real light, and not with the borrowed reflection of gifts. Common men are apologies for men; they bow the head, excuse themselves with prolix reasons, and appearances, because the substance is not.

—SPIRITUAL LAWS

Do you make excuses for not doing something you should? What would it mean to you to "be a gift and a benediction"?

There is throughout nature something mocking, something that leads us on and on, but arrives nowhere, keeps no faith with us. All promise outruns the performance. We live in a system of approximations. Every end is prospective of some other end, which is also temporary; a round and final success nowhere. We are encamped in nature, not domesticated. Hunger and thirst lead us on to eat and to drink; but bread and wine, mix and cook them how you will, leave us hungry and thirsty, after the stomach is full. It is the same with all our arts and performances. Our music, our poetry, our language itself are not satisfactions, but suggestions. The hunger for wealth, which reduces the planet to a garden, fools the eager pursuer. What is the end sought? Plainly to secure the ends of good sense and beauty, from the intrusion of deformity or vulgarity of any kind. But what an operose method! What a train of means to secure a little conversation! This palace of brick and stone, these servants, this kitchen, these stables, horses and equipage, this bank-stock, and file of mortgages; trade to all the world, country-house and cottage by the waterside, all for a little conversation, high, clear, and spiritual! Could it not be had as well by beggars on the highway? No, all these things came from successive efforts of these beggars to remove friction from the wheels of life, and give opportunity.... Unluckily, in the exertions necessary to remove these inconveniences, the main attention has been diverted to this object; the old aims have been lost sight of, and to remove friction has come to be the end.

—Nature

Have you followed a wayward path and lost track of the aims of life? How so?

DECEMBER

Meditations

DECEMBER 1

The reform that applies itself to the household must not be partial. It must correct the whole system of our social living. It must come with plain living and high thinking; it must break up caste, and put domestic service on another foundation. It must come in connection with a true acceptance by each man of his vocation,—not chosen by his parents or friends, but by his genius, with earnestness and love.

—DOMESTIC LIFE

What does "plain living and high thinking" mean to you?
What have you done to accomplish this?

DECEMBER 2

Do you not see that a man is but a bundle of relations, that his entire strength consists not in his properties, but in his innumerable relations? If you embrace the cause of right, of your country, of mankind, all things work with and for you, the sun and moon, stocks and stones. The virtuous man and the seeker of truth finds brotherhood and countenance in so far forth, in the stars, the trees, and the waters. All nature cries to him, All Hail! The bad man finds opposition, aversation, death in them all. All mankind oppose him. No whisper from secret beauty or grandeur cheers him. The world is silent; the heaven frowns.

—JOURNAL, 1836

Do you feel infinitely related? Do you find strength in a sense of kinship with all of life?

DECEMBER 3

At present, man applies to nature but half his force. He works on the world with his understanding alone. He lives in it, and masters it by a penny-wisdom; and he that works most in it, is but a half-man, and whilst his arms are strong and his digestion good, his mind is imbruted, and he is a selfish savage. His relation to nature, his power over it, is through the understanding; as by manure; the economic use of fire, wind, water, and the mariner's needle; steam, coal, chemical agriculture; the repairs of the human body by the dentist and the surgeon. This is such a resumption of power, as if a banished king should buy his territories inch by inch, instead of vaulting at once into his throne. Meantime, in the thick darkness, there are not wanting gleams of a better light,—occasional examples of the action of man upon nature with his entire force,—with reason as well as understanding.

—Nature

Do you think our approach to nature is largely utilitarian and rarely appreciative? What would happen if human beings were more appreciative of nature?

DECEMBER 4

These facts have always suggested to man the sublime creed, that the world is not the product of manifold power, but of one will, of one mind; and that one mind is everywhere active, in each ray of the star, in each wavelet of the pool; and whatever opposes that will, is everywhere balked and baffled, because things are made so, and not otherwise. Good is positive. Evil is merely privative, not absolute: it is like cold, which is the privation of heat. All evil is so much death or nonentity. Benevolence is absolute and real. So much benevolence as a man hath, so much life hath he. For all things proceed out of this same spirit, which is differently named love, justice, temperance, in its different applications, just as the ocean receives different names on the several shores which it washes. All things proceed out of the same spirit, and all things conspire with it. Whilst a man seeks good ends, he is strong by the whole strength of nature. In so far as he roves from these ends, he bereaves himself of power, of auxiliaries; his being shrinks out of all remote channels, he becomes less and less, a mote, a point, until absolute badness is absolute death.

— The Divinity School Address

Do you believe that the universe is the creation "of one will, of one mind"? How do you account for evil?

DECEMBER 5

[People] think that to be great is to possess one side of nature,—the sweet, without the other side,—the bitter. This dividing and detaching is steadily counteracted. Up to this day, it must be owned, no projector has had the smallest success. The parted water reunites behind our hand. Pleasure is taken out of pleasant things, profit out of profitable things, power out of strong things, as soon as we seek to separate them from the whole. We can no more halve things and get the sensual good, by itself, than we can get an inside that shall have no outside, or a light without a shadow. "Drive out nature with a fork, she comes running back." Life invests itself with inevitable conditions, which the unwise seek to dodge, which one and another brags that he does not know; that they do not touch him;—but the brag is on his lips, the conditions are in his soul....So signal is the failure of all attempts to make this separation of the good from the tax, that the experiment would not be tried,—since to try it is to be mad,...so that the man ceases to see God whole in each object, but is able to see the sensual allurement of an object, and not see the sensual hurt; he sees the mermaid's head, but not the dragon's tail; and thinks he can cut off that which he would have, from that which he would not have.

—COMPENSATION

Have you tried to separate the sweet in life from the bitter? Were you successful?

Thus there is no sleep, no pause, no preservation, but all things renew, germinate, and spring. Why should we import rags and relics into the new hour? Nature abhors the old, and old age seems the only disease; all others run into this one. We call it by many names,—fever, intemperance, insanity, stupidity, and crime; they are all forms of old age; they are rest, conservatism, appropriation, inertia, not newness, not the way onward. We grizzle every day. I see no need of it. Whilst we converse with what is above us, we do not grow old, but grow young. Infancy, youth, receptive, aspiring, with religious eye looking upward, counts itself nothing, and abandons itself to the instruction flowing from all sides. But the man and woman of seventy assume to know all, they have outlived their hope, they renounce aspiration, accept the actual for the necessary, and talk down to the young. Let them, then, become organs of the Holy Ghost; let them be lovers; let them behold truth; and their eyes are uplifted, their wrinkles smoothed, they are perfumed again with hope and power. This old age ought not to creep on a human mind. In nature every moment is new; the past is always swallowed and forgotten; the coming only is sacred. Nothing is secure but life, transition, the energizing spirit. No love can be bound by oath or covenant to secure it against a higher love. No truth so sublime but it may be trivial tomorrow in the light of new thoughts. People wish to be settled; only as far as they are unsettled is there any hope for them.

—CIRCLES

Do you "grizzle" a little each day? How do you overcome the inertia of old age?

'Tis the best use of Fate to teach a fatal courage. Go face the fire at sea, or the cholera in your friend's house, or the burglar in your own, or what danger lies in the way of duty, knowing you are guarded by the cherubim of Destiny. If you believe in Fate to your harm, believe it, at least, for your good. For, if Fate is so prevailing, man also is part of it, and can confront fate with fate. If the Universe have these savage accidents, our atoms are as savage in resistance. We should be crushed by the atmosphere, but for the reaction of the air within the body. A tube made of a film of glass can resist the shock of the ocean, if filled with the same water. If there be omnipotence in the stroke, there is omnipotence of recoil.

—FATE

What does it mean to confront fate with fate? Can you think of any examples?

Man begins to hear a voice...that fills the heavens and the earth, saying that God is within him, that *there* is the celestial host. I find that this amazing revelation of my immediate relation to God, is a solution to all the doubts that oppressed me. I recognize the distinction of the outer and the inner self,—of the double consciousness,—as, in the familiar example, that I may do things that I do not approve; that is, there are two selfs, one which does or approves that which to other does not and approves not; or within this erring passionate mortal self, sits a supreme calm immortal mind, whose powers I do not know, but it is stronger than I am, it is wiser than I am, it never approved me in any wrong. I seek counsel of it in my doubts; I repair to it in my dangers; I pray to it in my undertakings. It is the door of my access to the Father.... It is the perception of this depth in human nature—this infinitude belonging to every man that has been born—which has given new value to the habits of reflexion and solitude. This has caused the virtue of independent judgment to be so much praised. This has given its odour to spiritual interpretations.

—SERMON 165

Do you sense an inner self or soul apart from your ego? Do you consult this inner self or soul as a source of answers and advice for dealing with the difficult problems of life?

DECEMBER 9

I need hardly say to anyone acquainted with my thoughts that I have no System. When I was quite young I fancied that by keeping a Manuscript Journal by me, over whose pages I wrote a list of the great topics of human study, as, *Religion*, *Poetry*, *Politics*, *Love*, *etc.* in the course of a few years I should be able to complete a sort of Encyclopedia containing the net value of all the definitions at which the world had yet arrived. But at the end of a couple years my Cabinet Cyclopedia though much enlarged was no nearer to a completeness than on its first day. Nay somehow the whole plan of it needed alteration nor did the following months promise any speedier term to it than the foregoing. At last I discovered that my curve was a parabola whose arcs would never meet, and came to acquiesce in the perception that although no diligence can rebuild the Universe in a model by the best accumulation or disposition of details, yet does the World reproduce itself in miniature in every event that transpires, so that all the laws of nature may be read in the smallest fact.

—JOURNAL, 1839

How would you describe the development of your own thought? What conclusions have you come to?

DECEMBER 10

The spiritual power of man is twofold, mind and heart, Intellect and morals; one respecting the truth, the other the will. One is the man, the other the woman in spiritual nature. One is power, the other is love. These elements always coexist in every normal individual, but one predominates. And as each is easily exalted in our thoughts till it serves to fill the universe and become the synonym of God, the soul in which one predominates is ever watchful and jealous when such immense claims are made for one as seem injurious to the other. Ideal and practical, like ecliptic and equator, are never parallel. Each has its vices, its proper dangers, obvious enough when the opposite element is deficient. Intellect is skeptical, runs down into talent, selfish working for private ends, conceited, ostentatious and malignant. On the other side the clear-headed thinker complains of souls led hither and thither by affections which, alone, are blind guides and thriftless workmen, and in the confusion asks the polarity of intellect. But all great minds and all great hearts have mutually allowed the absolute necessity of the twain.

—NATURAL HISTORY OF INTELLECT

How are the mind and heart balanced in your life? Does one or the other predominate? Which one?

DECEMBER 11

Action is with the scholar subordinate, but it is essential. Without it, he is not yet man. Without it, thought can never ripen into truth....Only so much do I know, as I have lived. Instantly we know whose words are loaded with life, and whose not....So much only of life as I know by experience, so much of the wilderness have I vanquished and planted, or so far have I extended my being, my dominion. I do not see how any man can afford, for the sake of his nerves and his nap, to spare any action in which he can partake. It is pearls and rubies to his discourse....It is the raw material out of which the intellect moulds her splendid products. A strange process too, this, by which experience is converted into thought, as a mulberry leaf is converted into satin.

—The American Scholar

Is your religion active? How do you keep it active?

DECEMBER 12

The lesson is forcibly taught by these observations, that our life might be much easier and simpler than we make it; that the world might be a happier place than it is; that there is no need of struggles, convulsions, and despairs, of the wringing of the hands and the gnashing of the teeth; that we miscreate our own evils. We interfere with the optimism of nature; for, whenever we get this vantage-ground of the past, or of a wiser mind in the present, we are able to discern that we are begirt with laws which execute themselves.

—Spiritual Laws

Do you make your life harder than it has to be? Do you believe in "the optimism of nature"?

DECEMBER 13

There is no power of expansion in men. Our friends early appear to us as representatives of certain ideas, which they never pass or exceed. They stand on the brink of the ocean of thought and power, but they never take the single step that would bring them there. A man is like a bit of Labrador spar, which has no luster as you turn it in your hand, until you come to a particular angle; then it shows deep and beautiful colors. There is no adaptation or universal applicability in men, but each has his special talent, and the mastery of successful men consists in adroitly keeping themselves where and when that turn shall be oftenest to be practiced. We do what we must, and call it by the best names we can, and would fain have the praise of having intended the result which ensues. I cannot recall any form of man who is not superfluous sometimes. But is not this pitiful? Life is not worth the taking, to do tricks in.

— EXPERIENCE

How might we take the step that would bring us to "the ocean of thought and power"? What "particular angle" shows the most beautiful colors in you?

DECEMBER 14

All ages of belief have been great; all of unbelief have been mean. The Orientals believe in Fate. That which shall befall them is written on the iron leaf; they will not turn on their heel to avoid famine, plague or the sword of the enemy. That is great, and gives a great air to the people. We in America are charged with a great deficiency in worship; that reverence does not belong to our character; that our institutions, or politics and our trade have fostered a self-reliance which is small, lilliputian, full of fuss and bustle; we look at and will bear nothing above us in the state, and do exceedingly applaud and admire ourselves, and believe in our senses and understandings, while our imagination and our moral sentiment are desolated. In religion too we want objects above; we are fast losing or have already lost our old reverence; new ideas of inspiration, of miracles, of the saints, have supplanted the old opinions, and it is vain to bring them again. Revolutions never go backward, and in all churches a certain decay of ancient piety is lamented, and all threatens to lapse into apathy and indifferentism. It becomes us to consider whether we cannot have a real faith and real objects in lieu of these false ones. The human mind, when it is trusted, is never false to itself. If there be sincerity and good meaning. . .we shall not long look in vain.

— THE SOVEREIGNTY OF ETHICS

Would you say that ours is an age of belief or of unbelief? Do you think we can have "a real faith and real objects" in lieu of false ones?

DECEMBER 15

You shall not go to the sermons in the churches for the true theology, but talk with artists, naturalists, and other thoughtful men who are interested in verities, and note how the idea of God lies in their minds; not the less, how the sentiment of duty lies in the heart of the "bobbin-woman," of any unspoiled daughter, or matron, in the farmhouse. These are the crucial experiments, these the wells where the coy truth lies hid.

I think, as I go, Life is always rich; spontaneous graces and forces elevate it, in every domestic circle, which are overlooked, whilst we are reading of something less excellent in old authors. I go through the streets; each one of these innumerable houses has its own calendar of domestic saints, its unpublished anecdotes of courage, of patience, of wit, of cheerfulness. For the best, I know, were in the most private corners.

Everything draws to its kind, and frivolous people will not hear of noble traits; but let any good example of this secret virtue come accidentally to air, like Florence Nightingale, and you shall hear of parallel examples in every direction. From the obscurity and casualty of those which I know, I infer the obscurity and casualty of the like balm, and consolation, and immortality in a thousand homes which I do not know, and all 'round the world. Let it lie hid in the shade there from the compliments and praise of foolish society: it is safer so. All it seems to demand, is, that we know it, when we see it.

—THE RULE OF LIFE

Can you think of any examples of remarkable nobility that have gone unrecognized? How would you name the secret virtues, the ones you try to cultivate in yourself and look for in the actions of others?

Why unsettle or disturb a faith which presents to many minds a helpful medium by which they approach the idea of God?...It is because I think the popular views of this principle are pernicious, because it does put a medium, because it removes the idea of God from the mind. It leaves some events, some things, some thoughts, out of the power of Him who causes every event, every flower, every thought. The tremendous idea...of God is screened from the soul. Men are made to feel as if they ate their dinner and committed their common sins somewhere in the purlieus of the creation behind a screen, for the Spirit of God works in a church, or in Judea, and not in the vulgar affairs of every day. The Spirit of God teaches us, on the contrary, that not a star rolls in space, that not a pulse beats in a single heart, not a bird drops from the bough, not an atom moves throughout the wide universe but is bound in the chains of his Omnipotent thought—not a lawless particle. And least of all can we believe—Reason will not let us—that the Presiding Creator commands all matter and never descends into the secret chambers of the Soul. There he is most present. The soul rules over matter. Matter may pass away like a mote in the sunbeam, may be absorbed into the immensity of God as a mist is absorbed in the heat of the sun; but the Soul is the kingdom of God: the abode of love, of truth, of virtue. The bringing all minds into union with him is the work which god worketh from age to age.

—JOURNAL, 1831

In your own faith, is God part of the world or separate from it? Do you believe, as Emerson does, that "the soul is the kingdom of God"?

'Tis one of our first illusions, this belief in multitude, and it takes a long experience to disabuse us. We believe we see countless hosts of stars in the midnight firmament, but when counted, one by one, we do not make ten hundred. We talk of the multiplicity of our affairs, of the loss of acquaintances, of volumes of letters, of libraries of books, but we spend the most of our life in the company of a few persons; a principle of order reduces our affairs to an easy routine. We write more letters than we need and could easily write more. And so with all life; there is much noise, confusion, and chatter, but the net result of each day is a quite moderate amount. We talk of the variety of influences, of the variety of characters, of the conflict of principles, of the education of all the virtues, and life looks large, duty manifold, the future confused. Is it that there is some conspiracy to disconcert and embarrass us, and hide the simplicity of life? For really, as we grow older, we are struck with the steady return of a few principles. We are always finding new applications of the maxims and proverbs of the nursery: One old Bible is still enough to enunciate all the commandments for the most complex life in this giddy and arrogant century. Nay, a very small part of the book—a few chosen pages, a few golden rules—suffice for the guidance and comfort of the most advanced and advancing genius.

—ESSENTIAL PRINCIPLES OF RELIGION

Is life hopelessly complicated or essentially simple? How might you reduce the clutter and confusion of your life?

DECEMBER 18

Genius is very well but it is enveloped and undermined by Wonder. The last fact is still Astonishment, mute, bottomless, boundless, endless Wonder. When we meet an intelligent soul all that we wish to ask,—phrase it how we will,—is "Brother have you wondered? Have you seen the Fact?" To come out from a forest in which we have always lived, unexpectedly on the Ocean, startles us, for it is a symbol of this.

—JOURNAL, 1841

Have you wondered? Have you seen the fact? Have you ever been startled by reality?

We live by desire to live; we live by choice; by will, by thought, by virtue, by the vivacity of the laws which we obey, and obeying share their life,—or we die by sloth, by disobedience, by losing hold of life, which ebbs out of us. But whilst I find the signatures, the hints and suggestions, noble and wholesome,—whilst I find that all the ways of virtuous living lead upward and not downward,—yet it is not my duty to prove to myself the immortality of the soul. That knowledge is hidden very cunningly. Perhaps the archangels cannot find the secret of their existence, as the eye cannot see itself;—but, ending or endless, to live whilst I live.

— Immortality

What is your view of immortality? What do you live by and for?

In this kingdom of illusions we grope eagerly for stays and foundations. There is none but a strict and faithful dealing at home, and a severe barring out of all duplicity or illusion there. Whatever games are played with us, we must play no games with ourselves, but deal in our privacy with the last honesty and truth. I look upon the simple and childish virtues of veracity and honesty as the root of all that is sublime in character. Speak as you think, be what you are, pay your debts of all kinds. I prefer to be owned as sound and solvent, and my word as good as my bond, and to be what cannot be skipped, or dissipated, or undermined, to all the eclat in the universe. This reality is the foundation of friendship, religion, poetry, and art. At the top or at the bottom of all illusions, I set the cheat which still leads us to work and live for appearances, in spite of our conviction, in all sane hours, that it is what we really are that avails with friends, with strangers, and with fate or fortune.

—ILLUSIONS

Is honesty "the root of all that is sublime in character"? Do you find it difficult to be honest with yourself?

DECEMBER 21

The magnanimous know very well that they who give time, or money, or shelter, to the stranger—so it be done for love, and not for ostentation—do, as it were, put God under obligation to them, so perfect are the compensations of the universe. In some way the time they seem to lose is redeemed, and the pains they seem to take remunerate themselves. These men fan the flame of human love, and raise the standard of civil virtue among mankind. But hospitality must be for service, and not for show, or it pulls down the host. The brave soul rates itself too high to value itself by the splendor of its table and draperies. It gives what it hath, and all it hath, but its own majesty can lend a better grace to bannocks and fair water than belong to city feasts.

—HEROISM

Do you consider it heroic to be of service to others? Do you feel compensated in some way when giving time, money, or shelter to a stranger?

Patience and patience, we shall win at the last. We must be very suspicious of the deceptions of the element of time. It takes a good deal of time to eat or to sleep, or to earn a hundred dollars, and a very little time to entertain a hope and an insight which becomes the light of our life. We dress our garden, eat our dinners, discuss the household with our wives, and these things make no impression, are forgotten next week; but in the solitude to which every man is always returning, he has a sanity and revelations, which in his passage into new worlds he will carry with him. Never mind the ridicule, never mind the defeat: up again, old heart!—it seems to say,—there is victory yet for all justice; and the true romance which the world exists to realize, will be the transformation of genius into practical power.

—EXPERIENCE

Do you find sanity and revelations in solitude? Do you have confidence and optimism in spite of defeat and old age?

DECEMBER 23

A just thinker will allow full swing to his skepticism. I dip my pen in the blackest ink, because I am not afraid of falling into my inkpot. I have no sympathy with a poor man I knew, who, when suicides abounded, told me he dared not look at his razor. We are of different opinions at different hours, but we always may be said to be at heart on the side of truth. I see not why we should give ourselves such sanctified airs. If the Divine Providence has hid from men neither disease, nor deformity, nor corrupt society, but has stated itself out in passions, in war, in trade, in the love of power and pleasure, in hunger and need, in tyrannies, literatures, and arts,—let us not be so nice that we cannot write these facts down coarsely as they stand, or doubt but there is a counterstatement as ponderous, which we can arrive at, and which, being put, will make all square. The solar system has no anxiety about its reputation, and the credit of truth and honesty is as safe; nor have I any fear that a skeptical bias can be given by leaning hard on the sides of fate, of practical power, or of trade, which the doctrine of Faith cannot down-weigh.... We may well give skepticism as much line as we can. The spirit will return, and fill us. It drives the drivers. It counterbalances any accumulations of power.... We are born loyal. The whole creation is made of hooks and eyes, of bitumen, of sticking-plaster, and whether your community is made in Jerusalem or in California, of saints or of wreckers, it coheres in a perfect ball.

— Worship

Are you as comfortable as Emerson when it comes to the defense of faith against the negations of skepticism? How do you deal with your skepticisms?

DECEMBER 24

Everything good is the result of antagonisms, and the height of civilization is absolute self-help combined with most generous social relation. A man must have his root in nature, draw his power directly from it, as the farmer, miller, smith, shepherd, and sailor do....He must be such, that, set him down where you will, he shall find himself at home, shall see how he can weave his useful lines here as there, and make himself necessary to society by the method of his brain. This is self-help, and this is common. But the opposite element makes him, while he draws all values to him, feel an equal necessity to radiate or communicate all, and combine largest accumulation with bounteous imparting, and raise the useful to the heroic.

—Essential Principles of Religion

What antagonisms have led you to growth and creativity?
What do you have to "radiate or communicate" to others?

DECEMBER 25

Nature is not fixed but fluid. Spirit alters, moulds, makes it. The immobility or bruteness of nature, is the absence of spirit; to pure spirit, it is fluid, it is volatile, it is obedient. Every spirit builds itself a house; and beyond its house a world; and beyond its world, a heaven. Know then, that the world exists for you. For you is the phenomenon perfect. What we are, that only can we see. All that Adam had, all that Caesar could, you have and can do. Adam called his house, heaven and earth; Caesar called his house, Rome; you perhaps call yours, a cobbler's trade; a hundred acres of ploughed land; or a scholar's garret. Yet line for line and point for point, your dominion is as great as theirs, though without fine names. Build, therefore, your own world. As fast as you conform your life to the pure idea in your mind, that will unfold its great proportions. A correspondent revolution in things will attend the influx of the spirit. So fast will disagreeable appearances, swine, spiders, snakes, pests, madhouses, prisons, enemies, vanish; they are temporary and shall be no more seen.

—Nature

Do we build our own world? What kind of world are you building for yourself?

DECEMBER 26

Am I not, one of these days, to write consecutively of the beatitudes of intellect? It is too great for feeble souls, and they are over-excited. The wine-glass shakes and the wine is spilled. What then? The joy which will not let me sit in my chair, which brings me bolt upright to my feet, and sends me striding around my room, like a tiger in his cage, and I cannot have composure and concentration enough even to set down in English words the thought which thrills me—is not that joy a certificate of the elevation? What if I never write a book or a line? For a moment, the eyes of my eyes were opened, the affirmative experience remains, and consoles thorough all suffering. . . . I admire those undescribable hints that power gives of itself. I find sublime that essence of the man which makes him pass for more than his performances, though he never told his secret; is aware that a few private persons alone know him, and not one of them thoroughly.

—JOURNAL, 1859

Have you ever felt such joy that you could not sit still? Is there an essence of you known only to you and no one else?

The method of nature: who could ever analyze it? That rushing stream will not stop to be observed. We can never surprise nature in a corner; never find the end of a thread; never tell where to set the first stone. The bird hastens to lay her egg: the egg hastens to be a bird. The wholeness we admire in the order of the world, is the result of infinite distribution. Its smoothness is the smoothness of the pitch of the cataract. Its permanence is a perpetual inchoation. Every natural fact is an emanation, and that from which it emanates is an emanation also, and from every emanation is a new emanation. If anything could stand still, it would be crushed and dissipated by the torrent it resisted, and if it were a mind, would be crazed; as insane persons are those who hold fast to one thought, and do not flow with the course of nature.

—THE METHOD OF NATURE

What does the method of nature say about permanence in your life? Do you flow with the course of nature, or do you resist?

Man is timid and apologetic; he is no longer upright; he dares not say 'I think,' 'I am,' but quotes some saint or sage. He is ashamed before the blade of grass or the blowing rose. These roses under my window make no reference to former roses or to better ones; they are for what they are; they exist with God today. There is no time to them. There is simply the rose; it is perfect in every moment of its existence. Before a leaf-bud has burst, its whole life acts; in the full-blown flower there is no more; in the leafless root there is no less. Its nature is satisfied and it satisfies nature in all moments alike. But man postpones or remembers; he does not live in the present, but with reverted eye laments the past, or, heedless of the riches that surround him, stands on tiptoe to foresee the future. He cannot be happy and strong until he too lives with nature in the present, above time.

—SELF-RELIANCE

Do you live in the present? Do you spend time lamenting the past or fantasizing about the future?

Ineffable is the union of man and God in every act of the soul. The simplest person, who in his integrity worships God, becomes God; yet for ever and ever the influx of this better and universal self is new and unsearchable. It inspires awe and astonishment. How dear, how soothing to man, arises the idea of God, peopling the lonely place, effacing the scars of our mistakes and disappointments! When we have broken our god of tradition, and ceased from our god of rhetoric, then may God fire the heart with his presence. It is the doubling of the heart itself, nay, the infinite enlargement of the heart with a power of growth to a new infinity on every side. It inspires in man an infallible trust.

—THE OVER-SOUL

What does it mean to become one with God? Is the God in your heart different from the god of tradition and the god of rhetoric? How so?

DECEMBER 30

There is in woods and waters a certain enticement and flattery, together with a failure to yield a present satisfaction. This disappointment is felt in every landscape. I have seen the softness and beauty of the summer clouds floating feathery overhead, enjoying, as it seemed, their height and privilege of motion, whilst yet they appeared not so much the drapery of this place and hour, as forelooking to some pavilions and gardens of festivity beyond. It is an odd jealousy: but the poet finds himself not near enough to his object. The pine-tree, the river, the bank of flowers before him, does not seem to be nature. Nature is still elsewhere. This or this is but the outskirt and a far-off reflection and echo of the triumph that has passed by, and is now at its glancing splendor and heyday, perchance in the neighboring fields, or, if you stand in the field, then in the adjacent woods. The present object shall give you this sense of stillness that follows a pageant which has just gone by. What splendid distance, what recesses of ineffable pomp and loveliness in the sunset! But who can go where they are, or lay his hand or plant his foot thereon? Off they fall from the round world forever and ever. It is the same among the men and women, as among the silent trees; always a referred existence, and absence, never a presence and satisfaction.

—Nature

Do nature and life escape your grasp and seem just out of reach? Why do you suppose this is so?

DECEMBER 31

Thou shalt not profess that which thou dost not believe.

Thou shalt not heed the voice of man when it agrees not with the voice of God in thine own soul.

Thou shalt study and obey the laws of the Universe, and they will be thy fellow servants.

Nature shall be to thee as a symbol. The life of the soul in conscious union with the Infinite shall be for thee the only real existence.

Teach men that each generation begins the world afresh, in perfect freedom; that the present is not the prisoner of the past, but that today holds captive all the yesterdays, to judge, to accept, to reject their teachings, as they are shown by its own morning sun.

To thy fellow countrymen thou shalt preach the gospel of the New World, that here, here in America, is the home of man, that here is the promise of a new and more excellent social state than history has recorded.

> —Quoted in EMERSON: HOW TO KNOW HIM,
> By Samuel McChord Crothers

This passage, which may be apocryphal, summarizes Emerson's creed as a young man. How would you summarize your own creed? What are its basic principles?

EMERSON'S WRITINGS

The Complete Works of Ralph Waldo Emerson (Centenary Edition), Edward Waldo Emerson, ed., 12 vol., Houghton Mifflin, Boston, 1903.

The Complete Sermons of Ralph Waldo Emerson, Albert J. von Frank, et al., 4 vol., University of Missouri Press, Columbia, 1989–92.

The Early Lectures of Ralph Waldo Emerson, Robert E. Spiller, Stephen E. Whicher and Wallace E. Williams, eds., 3 vols., Harvard University Press, Cambridge, 1959-72.

The Journals and Miscellaneous Notebooks of Ralph Waldo Emerson, William H. Gilman, et al., ed., 16 vol., Harvard University Press, Cambridge, 1960-82.

The Later Lectures of Ralph Waldo Emerson, 1843–1871, Ronald A. Bosco and Joel Myerson, eds., 2 vol., University of Georgia Press, Athens, 2001.

The following excerpts are reprinted by permission of the Ralph Waldo Emerson Memorial Association and of Houghton Library, Harvard University: January 8, March 17, December 17, and December 24 entries from "Essential Principles of Religion," bMS Am 1280.207(4); January 16, February 23, March 25, and July 8 entries from "The Powers and Laws of Thought," Lecture I, *Mind and Manners of the Nineteenth Century*, bMS Am 1280.200(5); January 23 and February 15 entries from "Powers of the Mind," Lecture III, *Natural Method of Mental Philosophy*, bMS Am 1280.203(6); March 16 entry from Lecture IV, *Natural Method of Mental Philosophy*, bMS Am 1280.203(7); April 15 entry from "Reform," bMS Am 1280.205(10); April 23 entry from "The Relation of Intellect to Natural Science," Lecture II, *Mind and Manners of the Nineteenth Century*, bMS Am 1280.200(7); May 21, June 10, July 15, August 15, and September 13 entries from "Natural Religion," bMS Am 1280.205(13); May 26 and June 5 entries from "The Tendencies and Duties of Men of Thought," Lecture III, *Mind and Manners of the Nineteenth Century*, bMS Am 1280.200(10); July 4 entry from "American Slavery," bMS Am 1280.202(10); July 31 entry from "Perpetual Forces," bMS Am 1280.207(8); September 18 entry from "Address to the Citizens of Concord on the Fugitive Slave Law," bMS Am 1280.201(22); August 31 entry from "Perpetual Forces," bMS Am 1280.207(5); October 23 entry from "Moral Sense," bMS Am 1280.205(4); November 24 and December 15 entries from "The Rule of Life," bMS Am 1280.210(2); December 25 entry from "Economy," *Conduct of Life*, bMS Am 1280.201(24).